D0759105

Joyce
Joyce, J. D.
The story of rich : a
    financial fable of wealth
    and reason during
                        $40.00
                  ocn781681345
SM   01/30/2013

WITHDRAWN

Presented to

Spring Branch Memorial Library

By

**Karey Bresenhan In Memory of
Jewell Pearce Patterson**

Harris County
Public Library

your pathway to knowledge

Wiley Global Finance is a market-leading provider of over 400 annual books, mobile applications, elearning products, workflow training tools, newsletters and websites for both professionals and consumers in institutional finance, trading, corporate accounting, exam preparation, investing, and performance management.

www.wileyglobalfinance.com

Additional Praise for
The Story of Rich

"Joyce nicely weaves together the joy and difficulties of family life while educating readers on financial decisions."

> —Wayne Bohannon, CEO, Air Liquide
> Healthcare America

"I thought the book did great job of capturing the emotion of Rich's retirement and selling his business."

> —Bob Gardner, former president, Texas
> Mortgage Bankers Association

"Money managers will want to give this book to their new clients and probably some existing clients, so they can experience Rich's investment journey."

> —Henry Houston, former board
> chairman, Rosetta Resources, Inc.

"I found the novel captivating and well written without sacrificing the quality of the financial planning advice."

> —Richard C. Johnson, former managing
> partner, Baker Botts LLP (retired)

"Remarkably insightful book! As a passionate running coach and marathoner, I appreciate the parallels J.D. draws between investing and training for a marathon. Thanks, J.D., for proposing a fresh, new way to manage my financial life."

> —Debbie Mercer, director, USA FIT

"Investment planning is intimidating to most. *The Story of Rich* demystifies these principles in a relatable way. Those thinking about their financial future should get to know Rich Viva."

—David A. Miller, chief financial officer,
Valencia Group

"A stimulating read for any investor who wants to expand his or her knowledge."

—Carroll W. Phillips, CPA

The Story of Rich

The Story
of Rich

*A Financial Fable of
Wealth and Reason during
Uncertain Times*

J.D. Joyce
with Matt Joyce

WILEY

John Wiley & Sons, Inc.

Copyright © 2012 by John David (J.D.) Joyce. All rights reserved.

Published by John Wiley & Sons, Inc., Hoboken, New Jersey.
Published simultaneously in Canada.

No part of this publication may be reproduced, stored in a retrieval system, or
transmitted in any form or by any means, electronic, mechanical, photocopying,
recording, scanning, or otherwise, except as permitted under Section 107 or 108 of the
1976 United States Copyright Act, without either the prior written permission of the
Publisher, or authorization through payment of the appropriate per-copy fee to the
Copyright Clearance Center, Inc., 222 Rosewood Drive, Danvers, MA 01923, (978)
750-8400, fax (978) 646-8600, or on the Web at www.copyright.com. Requests to the
Publisher for permission should be addressed to the Permissions Department, John
Wiley & Sons, Inc., 111 River Street, Hoboken, NJ 07030, (201) 748-6011, fax (201)
748-6008, or online at www.wiley.com/go/permissions.

Limit of Liability/Disclaimer of Warranty: While the publisher and author have used
their best efforts in preparing this book, they make no representations or warranties
with respect to the accuracy or completeness of the contents of this book and
specifically disclaim any implied warranties of merchantability or fitness for a particular
purpose. No warranty may be created or extended by sales representatives or written
sales materials. The advice and strategies contained herein may not be suitable for your
situation. You should consult with a professional where appropriate. Neither the
publisher nor author shall be liable for any loss of profit or any other commercial
damages, including but not limited to special, incidental, consequential, or other
damages.

For general information on our other products and services or for technical support,
please contact our Customer Care Department within the United States at
(800) 762-2974, outside the United States at (317) 572-3993, or fax (317) 572-4002.

Wiley also publishes its books in a variety of electronic formats. Some content that
appears in print may not be available in electronic books. For more information about
Wiley products, visit our web site at www.wiley.com.

Library of Congress Cataloging-in-Publication Data:
Joyce, J. D., 1967–
    The story of rich : a financial fable of wealth and reason during uncertain times /
J.D. Joyce with Matt Joyce
        p. cm.
    Includes bibliographical references and index.
    ISBN 978-1-118-39014-6 (cloth); ISBN 978-1-118-42192-5 (ebk);
    ISBN 978-1-118-43427-7 (ebk); ISBN 978-1-118-41778-2 (ebk)
        1. Investments. 2. Wealth. I. Joyce, Matt, 1977– II. Title.
    HG4515.J69 2012
    332.024–dc23

                                        2012017379

Printed in the United States of America

10 9 8 7 6 5 4 3 2 1

To my family—Robyn, Allyson, and Ashley. The three of you give me a reason to smile. God has truly blessed me.

To my private clients, many of whom I consider friends. You make work meaningful and each day fun.

Contents

Foreword   ix
Preface   xvii
Acknowledgments   xxi

Chapter 1: Meet the Vivas   1

Chapter 2: Investment Plan   13

Chapter 3: Goals, Planning, and National Parks   27

Chapter 4: Goals and Objectives   39

Chapter 5: Risk Tolerance   53

Chapter 6: Asset Allocation and Meritage   67

Chapter 7: Mechanics of Investing and Winemaking   79

Chapter 8: The Marathon Runner and Time Horizon   95

Chapter 9: Cash Flow   111

Chapter 10: Trusted Advisor   125

Chapter 11: News versus Noise   135

CONTENTS

Chapter 12: Family Dynamics   149

Chapter 13: Estate Planning   159

Epilogue   171
About the Authors   185
Index   187

Foreword

The business schools at Northwestern University and The University of Chicago have teamed up to calculate and publish a Financial Trust Index. In March 2009, just after the Index was started, only 13 percent of people surveyed had trust in the stock market. This wasn't a surprise—it was the rock-bottom of the financial crisis. Across the country and around the world, couples were sitting down, reviewing their financial statements, and saying "well, at least we have each other." From a financial perspective, it seemed like there would soon be nothing else left.

At the other extreme, in 1999, at the height of the dot-com Nasdaq stock market boom, the Chicago/Northwestern Index did not exist. But if it had, the survey would probably have found that at least 75 percent of the country trusted the stock market. Remember those television commercials about "money coming out of the wazoo" and tow truck drivers buying their own personal islands? Real people were quitting their jobs to become day traders. Everyone could get rich trading stocks . . . or so many thought.

Isn't this interesting? The stock market crashed in early 2000, just when everyone thought getting rich was easy. And then, in March 2009, at the very bottom of the crisis, when no one thought stocks were safe, the market stopped going down, turned around, and climbed by 100 percent in two years.

In other words, if you find yourself going with the flow and agreeing with the masses, you may be making a huge mistake. In my 30 years of forecasting, speaking, and writing about the economy, what I have learned is that most people "buy high" and "sell low." When people are left to their own devices, most go with the flow and allow their emotions to take over. This is obviously a huge mistake.

Markets go through cycles, and those cycles generate volatility in emotions. It is the volatility in emotions, not the volatility in markets, that makes successful investing so difficult. That's why a financial advisor is so important and why this book is essential. Not that any financial advisor has the magical power to know when the market is high and when the market is low, but because a well-grounded financial advisor who understands your specific needs can keep you from making major mistakes. Good financial advisors are worth their weight in gold, and this book, if you take time to understand its nuances, is worth its weight in platinum. I am so glad J.D. Joyce took the time to write it.

What Do You Have Time For?

Successful doctors, contractors, and small business owners doing everything from baking great scones, to growing tasty strawberries, to making duck calls for hunters are all really, really good at what they do. If they weren't, they wouldn't be successful. Teachers, nurses, and landscapers are really, really good at what they do to. Nuances, tricks of the trade, and just plain old experience are things that cannot be taught easily and can't be bought. They come with hard work, thought, and just plain old time in the saddle. As we get older, we understand this more and more.

So if we understand this about carpentry, winemaking, and dentistry, why do so many people think that they can handle their financial needs without help? Isn't this like trying to perform surgery on yourself or program your own computer? I'm not saying it can't be done, but removing your own gall bladder while under anesthesia seems like it would be very hard to do.

That's why the experience of a good financial advisor is so valuable. The advisor lives, breathes, and wrestles with the infinite complexity of financial markets 24 hours a day, seven days a week. While you are reading the latest research on the efficacy of thyroid medication or deciding whether to use a brand new insulation material, your financial advisor is studying how inflation affects the equity-based closed-end mutual fund. Adam Smith, the father of modern economics, taught all of us the benefit of the specialization of labor. The economy is much more efficient when people focus on what they do best.

But there's more to being a financial advisor than just knowing things about financial products and markets. Good financial advisors like J.D Joyce are part-time psychologists, too. In other words, they have a much better chance of stopping you from "buying high" and "selling low" than you do. More importantly—and this is the main reason *The Story of Rich* is so important—the financial strategy you employ depends on your goals, personality, life history, and tolerance for risk. Everyone is different, and a good financial advisor will help design a financial plan that works for you.

Again, there are no clairvoyant financial advisors. But a good one will become your confidant and friend, the person who thinks about your future so that you can focus on what you do best, on your family, and on your legacy.

To paraphrase one of my favorite economists, Ludwig von Mises, government bonds were first invented by wealthy business owners who wanted to retire and stop worrying about the rough and tumble world of business. Wouldn't it be great if the ups and downs that we fight through in our working life could just go away when we retire? If we could just invest in one thing and not ever worry again? Wow . . . that would be relaxing. Unfortunately, it doesn't exist.

Imagine if you were a Greek citizen who bought Greek government debt and then the country defaulted. It wasn't so safe, now was it? But a default is not the only thing you have to worry about. Inflation erodes the value of debt, too. Gold works sometimes. It soared from 1973 to 1981, and again from 2001 to 2011. But it fell from

$800/ounce in 1981 to $255/ounce in 2001. What do the next 10 or 20 years hold?

This is the point: there are no perfectly safe, 100-percent guaranteed investments. You can't ever relax completely, but a good financial advisor can show you how to build a portfolio that fits your personality, minimizes your potential risk, and helps you achieve your goals.

Information Overload

All of this has become hyper-important these days. Financial news is ubiquitous on television and in print. It's everywhere and all the time. It presents every different point of view imaginable, and after perusing it, we are left with nothing but jumbled emotions, possibly some fear, and no clear plan for the future.

One thing to remember about journalists is that they get rewarded (paid) for viewership or readership. The more people that tune in to or click on their stories, the more valuable they are to potential advertisers. As a result, they will always gravitate toward the extreme stories and reportage, not the benign.

The house that burned down last night or the person who had an auto accident on the way to work this morning are the lead stories, and if there are flames or wreckage to show, it's even better. What we don't hear about are the 99.9 percent of houses that didn't burn down or the fact that everyone else made it to work safely. If that was the news, we would be bored and turn it off. It's not the journalists' fault; it's human nature.

The same is true for business and financial news. The headlines are Bernie Madoff, Enron, and bankruptcies. But just as importantly, the financial news swings with the emotions of its viewers. Back in 1999 and 2000, there was little warning of eminent collapse. Day traders made up the viewership of financial news, and they didn't want to hear negativity. These days, the opposite is true. Negativity is so prevalent that anyone who speaks optimistically is considered a Pollyanna, or just a salesman.

Finally—and this is one of the underlying flaws of financial journalism—there are always two sides presented. Now, don't get me wrong, I am all for presenting the "other side" of a story. Propaganda is not what I am after. But when every story has a pro and a con, it leaves the impression that the world is split 50/50 on an issue, when, in fact, the experts are frequently not.

For example, in mid-2012 if you turned on the television and saw a debate about the economy, almost always you would see a bull and a bear. One economist would be predicting recession; the other one would not. But did you know that in June 2012, in the Wall Street Journal official survey of 50 economists, none were predicting a negative quarter of GDP growth in 2013? In other words, all those bull/bear debates, which make it look like a recession is a 50/50 proposition, misrepresent the position of professional economists.

In other words, watching the financial news, which can be very informative, often leaves viewers with the impression that the future is much more dangerous than most professionals actually believe. And with thousands of sources for financial news (on the web and cable) available, it's information overload for the average viewer who has not spent their life paying attention to economic ideas and financial market history.

Now, I know what some of you are thinking at this point. This guy (the writer) is an economist and economists missed the collapse of 2008, didn't they? What does he know? Well, in a way, you would be right. Economists do not have a perfect track record, but then, who does? Listen to the experts about sports, or elections, or the weather. One thing all prognosticators have in common is that they will get it wrong.

If everything were easy and knowable, life would be boring. If there was no risk in life, it wouldn't be life. But this does not mean that we can't make decisions to minimize risk and maximize the potential to achieve our goals.

The Ongoing Crisis Mentality

And this brings us to what appears to be the most important issue facing investors and financial advisors these days. Was the Great

Recession – or Panic of 2008 – a watershed event that changed the future forever? Did it create a more dangerous economy? Did it prove that everything is a random walk? Does it mean planning has no value and advice no worth?

I don't think so. Economics is the study of human action. It is the study of how markets work and how people respond to incentives. It is the study of how wealth is created . . . not bank account wealth . . . but living standards, economic assets and productive efficiency. Do you ever stop and become amazed at how living standards have improved in the past 100, 200 or 1000 years? The average person these days lives better than the Royalty of centuries before.

This is because human beings are relentless in their pursuit of a better life. No matter how bearish people are, no matter how many politically-minded people try to tell you the world is in a "new normal" or that it has entered a more dangerous part of history, this did not change in 2008. The world has been through crises like the recent one many times before.

In the early 1980s, U.S. unemployment was 10.8 percent, inflation and interest rates soared, the savings and loan industry collapsed, every Latin and South American country (except for Colombia and Chile) defaulted on its debt, and pessimism was rampant. In 1989, Japan, then the second largest economy in the world and the most important trading partner of the U.S., hit a brick wall economically. But, the stock market and economy soared in the 1980s and 1990s. In other words, when you hear about Europe and China these days and people say the future is bleak, please remember that we have lived through this before.

And be very careful about letting your politics interfere with your investment decisions. If you are a liberal, you may be certain that if the government doesn't spend more, another recession is likely. If you are conservative, you may be certain that the government has already made so many mistakes that a new collapse is virtually guaranteed. When we let politics influence our investment decisions, we make huge mistakes. The stock market soared under both Ronald Reagan (a Republican) and Bill Clinton (a Democrat). A financial advisor can help you avoid those emotional and political biases.

Sit Back and Relax

Through the story of Rich and Peg Viva—imaginary, but very realistic clients—and their friends, J.D. Joyce elucidates the value of financial planning and a financial advisor. Like a great doctor, a financial advisor with a good "bedside manner," knowledge of markets, and an understanding of human emotions can make all the difference. Do you want a more enjoyable life? Do you want to be able to sit back and relax as much as possible? This book will teach you about markets and financial risk, but more importantly, it will teach you how your emotions and life decisions need to work holistically with your financial planning to create a better life.

Read it, and let it set you on a better course.

Preface

For nearly two decades, I've had the privilege of working closely with investors as they've navigated through uncertain times in the economy, the markets, and their personal lives. The best strategy we have for stability and long-term success in financial investing is a thoughtful investment plan. Investors who take planning seriously are better equipped to handle difficult times because their long-term view helps them to stay the course, rather than panicking and making rash decisions. This proactive strategy serves them well over time and typically results in less worry, greater long-term investment returns, and overall a better quality of life.

Unfortunately, not all investors buy into the idea of developing a long-term investment strategy based on logic and reason. This group tends to fly by the seat of their pants. The results are often anxiety, worry, and frustration with their portfolio performance. Sadly, those without long-term, grounded investment principles frequently succumb to volatility in the markets and make kneejerk reactions to short-term issues—decisions that can have long-term implications.

This book is for those wishing to learn more about developing an investment strategy that has the potential to last the test of time. By focusing on key steps used in developing an investment plan, these individuals will be able to base their investment decisions on logic, reason, and investment facts, not mere opinions and emotions. By determining what they are attempting to achieve before being in the heat of battle, they can rely upon these fundamental concepts when things don't go as planned in the economy and markets, or in their personal lives.

A new client once told me that he wished he had the ammunition to avoid making dumb mistakes in the past and that he was looking for someone to be able to talk him out of doing something foolish in the future. Obviously, I can't change the past. My goal is to assist my clients in establishing a sound investment plan and then provide enough factual data to help them avoid future pitfalls.

Believing that it is often easier and hopefully more entertaining to learn something through stories, I used fictional anecdotes to present the investment concepts outlined in this book. Our protagonist is Rich Viva, who recently sold his business and has come into considerable cash. Peg, his wife, has successfully handled the majority of investing in the past, but now, with more time, Rich also wants to be involved. The story follows Rich's journey as he learns about key investment concepts and the development of an investment plan from his daily experiences with old friends and new acquaintances.

For Rich, the sale of his business provided the impetus for him to learn more about investing. For others it may be retirement, rolling over an IRA, the death of a spouse, divorce, an inheritance, hitting the jackpot, or simply making enough money from one's profession. People in any of these situations will find advice on the key considerations and steps involved in building an investment plan to potentially meet their goals and objectives.

The advice in the book is applicable to anyone interested in learning more about fundamental investing concepts, whether they have a large net worth or not. The planning strategy can be applied to those in, or near, retirement and to those just starting their journey. Regardless of one's wealth, age, goals, or interests, long-term investment planning can be useful in helping readers live up to their dreams, goals, and objectives.

Investing is psychological. We humans tend to let our emotions dictate our investment decisions. My wife likes to joke that I'm a financial advisor and part-time, untrained therapist. Too often, we can be our own worst enemies when it comes to making wise investment decisions. A good investment plan can provide assistance when we are most in need of guidance.

I am not clairvoyant, nor do I claim to be. However, I believe that most investors would have greater results if they developed a plan that clearly targets their goals and objectives. This book provides step-by-step guidance on the key ingredients needed to formulate a plan. However, I highly recommend that investors consult with a financial advisor. I am not qualified to offer tax or legal advice. Investors should consult with an attorney and/or a certified public accountant as their specific needs warrant.

Some of my clients will be guessing what role they play in this book. Fear not; every character in the book is a figment of my imagination, and they do not represent specific individuals. Each character and personality is an amalgamation of investors with whom I've worked over the years.

My hope is that anyone who reads this book and takes it to heart will be a more competent, less worried, and more successful investor. My goal is that the stories in this book will help bring you more happiness and success.

Acknowledgments

All through my life, I've been blessed to know people who have shown me the way and have taught me what to do and how to do it. I will be forever thankful to God for putting these people in my life.

Writing this book has taken dedication, hard work, and long hours. Without my cousin Matt, this book would not be a reality. Thank you to Matt Joyce—a reporter, a writer, and a good friend. Matt, even if the book never came to fruition, the endeavor would have been worthwhile simply to have gotten to know you.

To the many who assisted with background data and expertise, I thank you. Dr. Jim Jackson and Reverend Bob Johnson of Chapelwood United Methodist Church, thank you for your input on Proverbs. To Dr. Fred Smeins, thank you for your input on land management and ecology. Thanks also to Fred and Judy Smeins for opening their lake house for writing meetings. Thanks to Dave Jacobson for the introduction to David Reynolds of Leona Valley Winery. Thank you, David, for your time and expert advice on wine and wine making and how it relates to investing. To Scott Morrison and Rachel Leneham of the law firm Oaks, Hartline & Daly: Your advice on estate planning is very much appreciated. To Carrie Hoye: Your expert advice on business development and step-by-step direction is priceless.

To my wife and daughters: Thank you for tolerating my demanding work schedule, and for allowing me the extra time I needed on nights and weekends to write a book. Thank you for your understanding. Robyn, you are the love of my life and one incredible woman! You bring balance and reason and serve as a constant reminder of what it's all really about. What did I ever do to deserve you? Allyson and Ashley, you are gifts from God. You've been blessed with everything needed to make it in life. It will be fun seeing what you choose to accomplish. Whatever it is, I know it will be amazing and will be the right thing for each of you.

To my Mom and my Dad: Through your examples I learned the meaning of hard work. You instilled a drive and work ethic in me from an early age, and for this I am forever grateful.

To my three older brothers, Jeff, Glenn, and Jim: Growing up I always benefited from the halo effect and being your younger brother. Thank you for a good name—it's worth more than gold. Jeff, your legal advice is worth more than any fee. Your regular pro bono assistance is almost too good to be true. Glenn, the wisdom you share and your outlook on life are greatly appreciated. My favorite tidbit from you is that if a problem is financial, it's not truly a problem. Jim, you've always been there helping me. From the Sno-cone stand to the hammock design, you've been there to make it happen. I enjoy our time together.

To Bill Hobson, my retired business partner: Hobson, I'm the beneficiary of the 30-plus years you spent building up our practice. You have been a mentor, friend, confidant, and associate who I will always admire and respect. You are a good man, and I am better for having known you.

To my private clients and friends: I appreciate you, your business, and the confidence you place in me. Thank you for entrusting your life savings to me. This responsibility is not taken lightly. It is an honor to plan, direct, monitor, and evaluate your portfolio and to implement strategies to work toward your goals and objectives. Thank you for letting me be part of your life. It is a privilege.

To my colleagues, associates, and former colleagues who made this a reality: Thank you to Katie Tucker Letsos, who keeps everything working at the office. Your attention to detail and perfect execution make life much less stressful. To Dell Thomason, thank you for your friendship over the years and for researching various issues with keen insight and understanding. I appreciate what both of you do daily to serve our clients, and I thank you for all you did to make this book a reality. I'd like to thank the late Davis McGill for the time he spent teaching me about investing my money from mowing lawns as a teen. This was the genesis of my interest in investing. To Chuck Albanese: I was but a stranger when you opened your home and office countless times for me to pursue my New York adventure. Your generosity, kindness and frienship are greatly appreciated. To Tommy Orr, for seeing something in the young kid out of graduate school wanting to make it in the investment business: Thanks for hiring me and for the opportunity. To Shayne Berry and Ann Page: I am so appreciative of the time you spent in helping me develop as a financial advisor. To Chris Miller: Your management style and advice are invaluable, and I am fortunate to have you as a friend. To Jonathan Eisenberg, Mike Schweitzer, Sean Murphy, Ben Tarantino, Jim Starnes, Darryl Lipinski, Ann Fitzgerald-Salazar, and Patricia Sparks: You are all great partners. To our media relations group—both past and present—Karina Byrne, Allison Chin Leong, Emma Stradling, and Jason Shaw: Your understanding and support are awesome.

To Michael Ashton, your introduction to Bill Falloon was one of the best introductions I've ever had. To all those at Wiley, it has been great working with you. Bill Falloon, thank you for your willingness to take a chance on me. To Bill, Jen MacDonald, Steve Kyritz, Jodi Brandon, Sharon Polese, and Tiffany Charbonier, I appreciate all you've done to improve the book.

As the litany of names above shows, once again, I realize just how fortunate I am to have so many who have assisted me in achieving a life long goal of writing a book. Thank you God for always watching over me and, in spite of my many mistakes, still making everything work out!

Matt wishes to thank J.D. for the opportunity and his dedication to the project, the experts who shared their knowledge, and Vanessa and Corina for their support and patience.

Chapter 1

Meet the Vivas

"What now?" Rich glanced at his reflection in the rearview mirror of his silver SUV as he backed out of the parking garage at his attorney's office. He had just inked the deal of a lifetime: the sale of his company—the fruit of his years of hard work—to a competitor. His profit: $12 million after tax. "Who'd have thought a mechanical engineer with a knack for building air compressors could have pulled this off?" Rich was on top of the world, but also felt a sense of doubt about whether he was making the right decision.

Richard Viva, 58, was a true success by almost any measure. He'd prospered in business, raised a healthy family, and built a strong reputation in the community. But on this day, the person he saw in the rearview mirror almost startled him.

He stepped on the brake and scanned his face. For some reason, for perhaps the first time in years, he took a hard look at himself. "I had no idea my hair had turned so gray," he almost said out loud. "And those creases on my forehead and face—when did they dig in?"

The fact that he had visibly grown older concerned him, and the fact that he had done so without noticing bothered him even more. After all, this transformation didn't exactly occur overnight.

"Man, if I didn't even recognize my own physical appearance changing in front of me, what else did I miss out on over the last 20 years?" Rich pondered. Interesting the things we focus on when we no longer have to worry about the day-to-day responsibilities of life's routines.

"Perhaps old Maslow had it right with his hierarchy of needs theory," Rich thought. Things were beginning to enter Rich's mind that he hadn't contemplated in the past. He'd been constantly preoccupied with business over the years, and besides, who had time to think about things such as this in today's hectic and fast-paced world?

Rich was at one of life's crossroads, leaving behind something comfortable and known for something unknown and uncertain. He knew one thing for sure: Life would be different from now on. He just hoped it would be different in a good way, not bad.

Rich had not lived without a paycheck since he left his parents' house. There had been lean times during his career, especially in the early days, but he could still count on regular income. That would be different now. The thought scared Rich. Twelve million dollars was a lot of money, but not an infinite supply. Could his family outlive their money? He realized he had a lot to learn about financial investing, and he didn't really know where to start.

For anyone aiming to invest wisely, the key to getting started would be to develop an investment plan. Rich would be well equipped to plan confidently for his family's future by identifying his goals and objectives, recognizing the level of risk he was comfortable with taking in his investments, determining his future cash flow needs, and setting a time frame for his plan. But as the magnitude of the business sale sunk in, Rich had not yet begun the journey of learning the principles of an investment plan and the comfort it would bring.

Rich was a self-made man when it came to business. He knew it would be up to him to define what would lie ahead. Much of life's outcome is based upon outlook. He needed a realistic and positive outlook to help shape and determine his future. Unbeknown to him, an investment plan would guide his path to investing success.

Rich recognized that so many years had passed so quickly—just disappeared. It seemed like just yesterday that he had opened Apex Compression Services, Inc. (ACS) in a metal-sided building on the outskirts of Houston. But in reality it was 22 years before, and life had flown by since then.

When he first left corporate America to pursue his entrepreneurial calling, it hadn't been by his own design. In fact, he had been part of a restructuring of a major public company. The "downsizing," as they now call it, was quite a blow. Rich had worked hard for the company, and he had never failed at anything in his life. But there he was at the age of 36 being asked to leave.

It seemed devastating at first, but it ended up being the push he needed to launch his own company. He tapped into his positive attitude and get-it-done spirit, which made it easier. And he was excited about being his own boss. He liked the idea of eating what he killed, and he knew he was hungrier than anyone he knew. Besides, he had a pregnant wife and a 3-year-old daughter at home, and it was up to him to support his family and to make ACS a success. The consequences for his family were too high to accept any other outcome. He would be a success, for he had no other choice but to make it work.

ACS made compressors that pushed oil and gas through gathering lines and pipelines to refineries. The business had grown steadily and managed to keep busy through the various booms and busts of the energy business. It almost seemed funny that today, ACS had higher revenues in one week than they had in the first two full years of business combined. Opportunity comes to those in the right place at the right time—and who are willing to sacrifice virtually everything to make it work. Rich enjoyed his work and thought of the business almost as a member of his family. For all intents and purpose, it was.

"Oil and gas companies are always going to need compressors to move their product," Rich liked to say. New wells call for new compressors to move the product to market; old wells call for compressors to compensate for a loss of natural pressure.

Rich was always looking for new business, and that served him well. Regardless of his success, he was driven to improve the company, its products, and its services. This drive afforded him and his family the lifestyle that they had come to know and enjoy.

As he drove along, Rich's mind wandered to a recent business meeting and a potential customer who would surely benefit from the products and services of ACS. Then it hit him: "I don't have to think about this anymore," Richard thought. ACS, pipeline compressors, and all that stuff were now the problem of those Oklahoma boys who had just written him a check—a 10-digit check.

"That chapter of life is over," he thought, "and now it's on to bigger and better things."

He thought about his family. The kids were grown and off to their own pursuits, worrying about their own problems. He questioned if he had been the dad he had hoped and planned to be. Those 22 years sure did fly by.

The kids had grown up with the company. When they were younger, they craved spending more time with him. The feeling was mutual, but the business put food on the table. Rich's choices seemed logical at the time. What was good for business was good for the family. So, when it came between time with the family and time making the company operate at its maximum capacity, Rich focused his attention on the company.

As the children grew older, he yearned to spend time with them, but they had grown conditioned to his schedule and his preoccupation with work. They knew their dad as the busy business owner. The dad who worked tirelessly, traveling frequently and always on the phone putting out fires at work. "They can't say I didn't work hard for them," Rich thought, "and I can't wait to reap the rewards with them."

Rich thought about his wife, Peg. She had worked really hard as well and had been part of the business since the beginning. She worked for ACS in the early days and occasionally still helped out around the office. Richard could always count on Peg to support him, the kids, and the business. Importantly, she served as a voice of reason and logic during times of uncertainty. She understood Rich's strengths and weaknesses and was a wonderful sounding board.

Peg had embraced her husband's life as a small business owner, and she accepted the toll it took on his time. There were sacrifices.

Vacations were rare. And on the occasions when they did get away to the mountains or the beach, Rich was frequently distracted by work issues back in Houston. With this came a lifestyle that few others would be able to afford. The Vivas enjoyed the finer things of life, but few with lesser means would understand the price paid to get to this level.

Rich thought about his success and the toll it had taken on his family—the long hours and constant distractions. "Thank goodness those days are over."

Rich looked forward to "doing right" by Peg—spending time with her, pursuing her interests, and making time for the travel plans that they had always put on the backburner.

He also wanted to spend more quality time with his kids. They were always a priority to Rich, but if measured by time, they may not realize it. Had it not been for Peg, the kids would not be who they are today. While Rich was busy building his company into a success, Peg was nurturing and guiding the children to successful, productive adulthoods. Peg had chaired virtually every school group one can imagine, and then some. She was mother extraordinaire and smart enough to serve as a senior vice president of any public company. When ACS first began, she knew Rich had no option but to work day and night to make it a success. As years went by, and the kids started school, she began volunteering at school and on various charity boards that made a difference to women and children in need.

The pattern became routine: Peg would volunteer, and soon her efforts would be recognized. The reward for service was greater responsibility. Ultimately, Peg chaired most organizations to which she dedicated her time and efforts.

Peg and Rich had a good relationship. Their comfort level with one another was high, as each recognized the other's strengths. They enjoyed one another's company and they complemented one another nicely. Over the years, they had lived through a lot together, and their love seemed stronger today than when they first met back in college.

Peg was kind, smart, and pretty. Her friends often described her as being as pretty on the inside as she was on the outside. In her 50s she still turned heads, and Rich enjoyed complimenting her college-like figure. They were good together and it was doubtful either would have gone as far in life without the other. Rich recognized that he was more successful at business because he knew matters at home were being cared for over the years, especially when the kids were younger. He felt comfort in knowing they were getting the best upbringing that any could have.

Peg could relate to Rich's uncertainty over the sale of the company. Rich had been too busy running the company to recognize it, but she had felt the same when the kids had left for college and they became empty-nesters. With the sale of ACS, Rich's baby had left him and he, too, would experience similar questions of self-worth and his own significance. There would be moments of regret. Rich was fortunate to have a woman like Peg in his life. She would be there to help sort out the next leg of life's journey.

Rich noticed a billboard advertisement for Southwest Airlines and began to think of traveling for pleasure. "Maybe we'll get a cabin in the Colorado mountains," Rich daydreamed, "or a beach house in Florida, or maybe even both. The sky's the limit."

Rich was a dreamer, and he dreamt about the possibilities. The idea of a vacation home seemed pretty extravagant. But then again, he knew several people who had second and third homes, and they didn't have the net worth of the Vivas. Maybe this time it wasn't a grandiose dream, but simply the reality of their financial success.

Goosebumps tickled Rich's arm. It wasn't the air-conditioning; it was pure, unbridled optimism. Rich flipped the radio to one of the country stations and sang along. Ironically, Kenny Rogers's classic "The Gambler" was playing.

The song was particularly relevant to Rich on this day. He knew that when something was in high demand, it was time to sell, and when something was in low demand, it was probably time to buy. With the shale gas boom sweeping the country, his company was in high demand. The timing was right.

Rich drove down the oak-lined streets of Houston, soaking it all in. He stopped at a red light at San Felipe, the same corner where his financial advisor had an office. Rich's longtime friend and financial advisor, Greg Webber, had died of a heart attack a few months earlier. It was a tough loss, personally and professionally. Rich had complete trust in Greg and had been counting on his help in updating his investment plan after the ACS sale went through.

"I wish Greg was still alive," Rich thought to himself. Greg was a good guy, but like Rich, he worked more hours than he probably should have. Greg knew he was managing his clients' life savings, and he was there during important times in their lives. Financial advisors and their clients often develop friendships and mutual respect.

Rich could recall many of the times Greg had provided truly good advice. He was not clairvoyant, but like Peg, he served as the voice of reason during emotional, perhaps even turbulent times in the market and in Rich's professional and personal life. The two of them knew one another well. Not only had Greg assisted Rich with key insights and investment advice, but they had also worked together on the finance committee at Houston's Grace Methodist Church, where they both were members. It seemed like just yesterday when the two of them had last met at one such meeting, only to be followed by a memorial service for Greg a week later.

While Rich and Greg were good friends, Greg had actually worked more frequently with Peg on the Vivas' finances. Rich was so busy running ACS that Peg had long ago taken over the personal finances at home. This worked well for the Vivas. Peg's investment acumen was strong, and Rich was able to focus on his business. Rich realized that in today's busy world, he could accomplish so much more in business with Peg running interference at home and with the family's finances.

Greg's death had made a big impact on Rich. Other than working long hours, Greg lived a relatively healthy lifestyle in today's busy world. The death of a peer caused Rich to think about his own mortality. Greg's death had actually provided another motivation for Rich to sell ACS: He only had one life to live, and he'd spent most of it on business. Maybe it was time for him to focus on the family and himself.

Rich's memories of Greg gave way to thoughts about financial planning. Rich was smart with money, but he wasn't an investment expert. Greg had constantly preached the virtues of financial planning, and thankfully, Peg adhered to much of it. Rich had grown his business through hard work, combined with a little bit of financial savvy and the good graces of luck. Mostly it was persistence and hard work.

Rich had always told his kids: There's not a problem that can't be solved by putting in a few more hours. He knew firsthand what hard work could bring, and he was always proud when his children's teachers commented on their work habits over the years. He had one consistent demand of his children, and that was that they work hard at whatever it was that they were doing. Although unorthodox, he didn't concern himself so much over the grades they received as long as they had worked hard. He also believed that good grades were the byproduct of hard work, so he figured that if they worked hard enough, it was likely to be reflected in their marks at school. Most of the time it was.

Rich practiced what he preached. No one could find fault with Rich's work ethic. Well, at least no one at the office. Even Horatio Alger would be proud. His grade for 22 years of hard work was a healthy income over the years, a lifestyle for his family that few could afford, and now the sale of his work accompanied by a wire of $12 million after tax! Now Rich was more convinced than ever of the link between hard work and success.

Rich thought investing was a different story, however. The markets answered to nobody. A guy from Houston with a portfolio of a few million bucks can basically only hope for the best and watch what happens, Rich thought. Although Rich knew this was not exactly accurate, and Greg and Peg had conveyed this to him time and time again, he still couldn't help feeling like he had very little control. Regardless of how hard he worked it, with passive investments he couldn't roll up his sleeves and drive out to the job site to fix the problem, like he could while running things at ACS.

Rich pulled onto the freeway and pointed his Mercedes SUV toward home. He and Peg had built a very comfortable lifestyle in the Memorial Villages of Houston. This enclave of six small, contiguous villages within the city limits of Houston offered everything a family could desire, with big lots, beautiful homes, and restaurants and shopping nearby. The Villages are small towns within the fourth-largest city in the nation. In the Villages, in many ways it feels as if one is located in the countryside, with all the conveniences of a major city within a few minutes' drive. En route to home he passed the defining features of much of Houston: the low-slung barbecue and seafood restaurants, the strip joints, the gleaming mega-churches, and the immaculate high-rise condo complexes. They all lined up next to one another in odd formation, like the characters in an awkward photo in the *Houston Chronicle*'s society pages. It could only happen in a big city with no zoning restrictions.

Rich believed in personal freedom and liberty like many of his fellow Texans, especially Houstonians, and that included the freedom to do what you want with your own property. But with most good things there are limits. The occasional skyscraper in the middle of a residential area raised the question: Could Houston have benefitted from better planning?

Those words bounced around in Rich's head: *better planning, better planning, better planning.* A nagging feeling emerged from Rich's stomach, climbed up his chest, and sat firmly on his shoulders.

Rich's bravado about the business sale had given some ground to the nagging questions and concerns that he had been trying to block out of his mind. For three decades, he had defined himself through his work in the energy business. He was the compression expert and owner of ACS Inc. Rich had few regrets about the way he conducted his business. His business associates admired him, and so did his competitors, so much so that he had served as the president of the Texas Association of Independent Oilfield Service Companies, and one of his competitors just bought the business.

"Now what?" Rich thought to himself. "Who's going to give a flip about a has-been businessman and irrelevant retiree?"

He had never felt this way about other retirees, so it was an illogical notion. But that didn't block the feeling. He had always been his harshest critic. "How can I prove myself by walking the dog around the neighborhood and occasionally playing bad golf? Besides, my part in the family is to be the provider. Peg has been the best wife a guy could ask for. Now what do I bring to the table?"

Rich's mood darkened. Retirement sounded nice, but how is it relaxing to feel directionless? All those years building the business, working from "can't to can't"—an old expression for working from dawn to dusk before the sun is out until after it has set. At what cost? Rich knew he was fortunate and, by almost any standard, he was successful. Relative to others, he had friends galore, a beautiful family, and a decent net worth. But he didn't have very many close friends, only one or two he really felt close to. His kids had moved away to start their own lives. Peg was endlessly supportive, but she had found ways to make friends and broaden her life over the years while Rich was working all the time. To some extent, Peg had built her own life while Rich was always working. Just because he was facing major changes in his day-to-day activities, it didn't mean she was ready to do the same.

And what about money? Twelve million dollars sounded like a lot, especially considering their total net worth closer to $16 million, but would it really be enough for him and Peg to live on? He felt lucky to feel healthy at age 58, and he knew others such as Greg would change places with him in a heartbeat, but what if he and Peg lived another 30 years, or even 40? Investing is supposed to be the wise thing to do, but how would he and Peg live without regular income? Did they have enough to live on for the rest of their lives? What about the kids?

"What have I done?" echoed in his head. He had already signed the contract; there was no turning back. "What on earth was I thinking?" Rich was feeling pretty nasty by that point. It's funny how one can go from popping the celebratory Champagne to feeling distraught.

Rich was having true seller's remorse. His crummy feeling only got worse as he spotted a homeless man asking for change at the corner. "How can I feel so rotten with all I have when there are people in the world who can't even eat today?" His guilt was making it worse. He thought about an article he'd read a few weeks earlier about how the poorest Americans were relatively rich compared to much of the world. He almost felt ashamed, but it didn't make him feel any better about his current situation. If anything, he felt a combination of gratefulness, confusion, and guilt—and guilt never made anything better that he knew of.

As the traffic light turned green, Rich's cell phone rang and flashed Ernie's name. Rich was relieved. He could use a diversion.

Ernie Troutman was Rich's college friend from Texas A&M. He was calling to check on the business sale meeting.

"What's up, buddy?" Ernie said. "Did you get it done?"

"Yeah," Rich said, his voice flat, "got it done."

"Congratulations! That's terrific!" Ernie said. "Why do you sound like your dog just got run over?"

"I don't know. I'm not sure what's wrong with me. I'm not a pessimist, Ernie, you know that, but I'm starting to question if this was a good idea," Rich said. "I now have no income and nothing to do."

Ernie chuckled. "Well, not to make you feel even worse, but I'm in a similar position and I couldn't be happier."

The irony of this was not lost on Rich. How could two people have very similar circumstances and yet see things so differently? "If only I could be more like Ernie," Rich thought, "at least when it comes to concern about financials and the future."

Ernie had a proposition: "You just need to get a new perspective and hopefully adjust to your new situation. I can't think of a better way to get a little perspective than spending a few days fly fishing with your old college buddy."

"Fly fishing?"

"Yeah, why don't we head to Jackson Hole this weekend and celebrate your newfound freedom with a few days of fly fishing in the mountains? Besides, I've seen you at times a lot worse than this. Remember during your sophomore year when—"

Rich interrupted Ernie's old war story. He didn't really want to be reminded of one of the many stupid things he had done in college, and secondly he was grasping for something that would help him relax and celebrate, so he jumped at the offer.

"Sounds like a plan," he said. "Sure, I can leave Saturday."

For the first time in decades his schedule was completely open. He hadn't been able to jump at a last-minute invitation like this since he was in college. Or, at least he always felt as if hadn't been able to do so.

Peg had plans to visit her sister in Austin for a few days, anyway. He would ask Peg to join him in Wyoming after the fishing trip with Ernie, and they could visit Yellowstone. Perhaps he could make up for the last time they visited the majestic area, the time he was holed up in a hotel room working on an ACS deal while the family went on with their daily activities without him. He recalled that wasn't the only "family vacation" that played out the same way, and he was determined to make up for all the lost time.

Besides, Ernie was a fun guy, and Rich could use some of his fun view of the world. This could be just what he needed. Fly fishing in the Tetons, one of the prettiest and most relaxing places on earth, with one of his oldest buddies would be fun.

"This trip may do the trick and get me thinking right," Rich thought.

Not only was Ernie fun to be around, he also knew a lot about investing.

"Now that I have all this cash lying around, I need to figure out what to do with it," Rich thought. "It needs to last a lifetime and with my trusted advisor six feet under, I feel a burden heavier than ever. Maybe I could learn a thing or two from Ernie."

Ernie's invitation was a welcome diversion, but Rich's concerns lurked in the back of his mind—concerns of identity, time, and money.

Chapter 2

Investment Plan

Rich flew into the Jackson Hole airport and picked up his rental Jeep in the parking lot. He drove toward the town of Jackson along the picturesque highway that bisects the valley called Jackson Hole. The Teton Range jutted into the sky on his right. To his left was the massive green valley that makes up the National Elk Refuge. He didn't spot any wildlife at first glance. Being early fall, most of the elk that wintered on the refuge were still out traversing the mountains.

Rich drove into town and stopped at a coffee shop to grab a cup of coffee. He knew he'd be able to get a solid cup of brew in Jackson, a town whose residents liked the best of everything. Rich had been to Jackson a couple of times before. He always wondered how the predominantly young population could afford to make a home there. For a small, remote town, Jackson was remarkably affluent and cosmopolitan. You could get great sushi, great coffee, great wine, craft beer—all those things that yuppies adore. Rich liked those amenities, too. Maybe he and Peg could buy a vacation home in Jackson Hole?

Maybe he could make friends with the area's most famous resident, Dick Cheney? Rich chuckled to himself. They were both veterans of the energy business, after all. Rich savored a sip of the extra-strong coffee and resumed his trip to the hotel in Teton Village where he would meet Ernie.

At the hotel, Ernie was enjoying a scotch on the rocks on an outdoor patio, gazing on the green forests and mountain peaks that stretched up from the valley. Ernie was eager to help his friend Rich enjoy retirement. Ernie knew that Rich could be a worrier. Rich had harnessed that trait to build ACS into a thriving business in an unpredictable industry. But Ernie hated to see his friend stress over retirement, a time when Rich should be focusing on peace and recreation. Rich's apparent concern about his financial situation struck Ernie as unfounded and most likely a product of irrational fear.

Ernie was rarely hampered by such concerns. He had a way of shaking off worries and enjoying the moment. A bon vivant with a taste for stogies and whiskey, Ernie adopted the life of fat-cat sportsman after he sold his construction firm. The firm provided construction services for oil companies that operated deepwater rigs, mostly in the Gulf of Mexico. He'd sold the company five years earlier, when he was 60. His timing was good; the price of oil was high and the BP Macondo well blowout and ensuing regulatory scrutiny had yet to transpire. Cash flow was not an issue for Ernie.

Ernie loved hunting and fishing, almost as much as he loved the plush lodges he lounged in while on trout-fishing expeditions in the Rockies, bighorn sheep hunts in Alaska, or duck-hunting trips in Argentina. He also loved women, especially new acquaintances. While he had settled down considerably from his wild days, Ernie had managed to go through three marriages and any number of girlfriends over a 40-year span. In fact, there was no telling how much Ernie would be worth had he not divided his estate a few times. Ernie had a good outlook on life and didn't have the time or inclination to spend pondering decisions of the past. Perhaps that was why he tended to make the same personal mistakes time and time again.

Ernie knew how to pay for the good life that he loved. He was a smart guy with serious business acumen. He loved to take risks during his business career, and not all had panned out. But he came out ahead in the end. Five years into his retirement, he had plenty of time to think about his finances, and he had taken an active role in protecting his financial future. He knew better than to take any more fool-hearted risks, at least when it came to business and investments. He also knew better than to spend his retirement worrying about his money. "If I can do it, surely Rich can," Ernie thought. "I need to convince him of this."

Rich found his buddy on the hotel patio, snoozing in his lounge chair in the mid-day mountain sun.

"Wake up, old man. The fish are biting."

Ernie opened one eye, stretched his arms, and picked himself up. They shook hands.

"Welcome to paradise, Rich. I've been waiting for you for several years now. I didn't know if you'd ever have the sense to join me."

The two went into the hotel to gather Ernie's fishing equipment. They chatted about the Texas weather and the relief of the mountains. They caught up on family goings-on back in Houston and plotted their fishing plan for the day.

Within an hour, Rich and Ernie were making their way down a steep embankment of the Snake River, just about a mile south of Jackson. A fishing guide had taken Ernie to the spot a few years before, and it had proved to be worthwhile. The next couple of hours were spent wading the river, casting lines for trout. Ernie pulled up a couple of fish and released them back into the river, as was the law in that area. Rich spent lots of time untangling his line.

"So have you found peace with your newfound life?" Ernie asked.

"Not exactly," Rich responded. "I mean, I'm thrilled with the business sale. I think I did about as well as I could have hoped on the deal. But I don't know if it was good enough to justify retirement. I guess it should've occurred to me earlier, but it's hard to imagine life without income. I mean, the financial advisor I met with the other day talked about updating our investment plan to account for the money Peg and I need to live on. I'm having a hard time seeing how we could possibly have enough."

Ernie perked up at the mention of an investment plan.

15

"An investment plan is the way to go. I revamped mine back when I sold my company five years ago. I learned a lot during that process. It gave me peace of mind."

"I thought you were born with peace of mind?" Rich said.

"Nobody's accused me of being a worrywart, this is true. But the investment plan didn't hurt."

Ernie ticked off the basic concepts he had considered when redrawing his investment plan five years earlier: goals and objectives, risk tolerance, time horizon, cash flow, asset allocation, mechanics of investing, the need to find wise and factual trusted advice, and the ability to recognize the difference between news and noise. When developing an investment plan, it is also a good idea for an investor to consider family dynamics and how the plan may impact others, including estate planning. All of these issues have a way of working together.

"Remember that great quote from Yogi Berra? 'If you don't know where you're going, you'll end up someplace else?'" Ernie asked. "That's what I think of when I think about goals and objectives.

"Think about what you want to do now that you have the freedom of retirement. Dream big. How about a vacation home? How about that six-month cruise around the world? At this point, the idea is to come up with what you would like to accomplish, not whether you can afford it," Ernie said. "Later, you'll put pen to paper to figure out if you can make it happen based upon how much money you have, how risky you're willing to be with your investments, and how much money you need over time."

"The first part sounds fun," Rich said. "Between Peg and me, I'm sure we can dream up some fun ways to spend money."

"Absolutely," Ernie said. "I certainly have excelled in that department. But making those dreams possible is where the rubber meets the road. The next investment concept to consider is what my advisor calls risk tolerance.

"In general, the more risk you take, the higher the potential return or loss. If you are ultra-conservative with your investments, then you probably should expect lower levels of volatility with your savings, but the result is lower returns over time. Only you and Peg really know the levels of volatility you are willing to accept. Usually, taking too much risk can make you feel bipolar; your emotions run from euphoria to depression depending on the market. On the other hand, if you take too little risk, you won't build your value. That can produce real problems in your old age if you outlive your money.

"I've tried to run the middle road. It offers the best of both worlds—an opportunity for a good return without the risk of losing the ranch."

"That seems reasonable," Rich said. "That really gets at the heart of my concerns. I don't want to be so worried about saving money that I stick the cash under my mattress. But I don't want to get carried away and lose it all in the market."

"You're a lot more even-keeled than I am," Ernie said, "and even I have found a risk balance that I'm comfortable with. The other thing you have to consider is how long you have to invest your money. My advisor calls it the time horizon."

"Generally, the longer you have, the more risk you can afford to take. As an example, if you are investing for your newborn grandchild to have enough money one day to pay for college, you can afford to take more risk. Even if a drop in your portfolio occurs, you have time to make it up. However, if she is now a junior in high school and you are in need of some of the savings for her first year of college, you really can't afford to take too much risk with this portion of the portfolio. You wouldn't have time to recover if your portfolio takes a hit during a pullback."

"That's one scary part of all this," Rich responded. "I've read about so many people who lost their retirement when the markets dropped during the recession. Now they're scraping by. I don't want to have to take a job as a greeter at Wal-Mart to make ends meet."

"But you would be so good at it," Ernie said. "I can just see it. I promise I would come buy bullets, propane, and fishing lures at your store."

"That's nice of you, but let's hope it doesn't get to that point," Rich said. "Speaking of lures, can you hand me a new fly?"

Ernie pulled a fly off his hat and handed it to Rich.

"Part of the way to stay out of that kind of trouble is to consider your cash flow needs," Ernie said. "This was probably the best advice I got from my advisor, because it gives me a cushion from the market swings.

17

"The idea of cash flow is to figure out how much money you need from your portfolio to subsidize your income stream.

"My advisor uses the term *cash flow ladder* to basically describe a savings account that sits beside my portfolio and where I keep enough cash to meet my needs. My cash flow is set up to cover about three years of cash needs, but you could reserve more from your portfolio if you want to be conservative. For example, let's say you and Peg need $100,000 a year from your portfolio and to play it safe, you reserve this amount to last for four years. You'll have $100,000 liquid for the first year and then invest another $300,000 in safe fixed-income holdings such as certificates of deposit—CDs—that mature on an annual basis. So then, regardless of gyrations in the market, you have plenty of cash to get by. You won't be forced to liquidate any of your portfolio during a pullback in the market. That's what happened to those retirees that you read about losing their savings.

"As part of the cash flow ladder, from time to time over the next four years, when part of your portfolio is doing well, you harvest some of those gains and add them to the ladder. Then you'll have time to accept the ups and downs of the market—hopefully without as much worry as the normal investor, because you have time on your side due to your ladder. Normally, your cash flow ladder doesn't offer much of a return but it provides cash when you need it.

"Also, using a cash flow ladder allows you to concentrate on growing the remainder of your portfolio because you're not preoccupied with your cash needs. However, holdings with a higher yield and that pay higher dividends can also help offset cash flow needs."

Ernie looked over and saw that Rich was wrestling with a good-looking rainbow trout.

"Hot damn! I knew you'd get one," Ernie said. "You been listening to me, or have I been talking to myself?"

"No. I heard you. I nearly let this fish get away because I was trying to picture a cash flow ladder in my head," Rich said. "I like the idea of setting aside cash so that not everything is tied up in the market."

"That's the idea," Ernie said. "By the way, my advisor basically said I can't withdraw more than about 4 percent of my portfolio per year, pretty much until my death. Otherwise, I would chip away at the portfolio to the point that it could never really appreciate."

Ernie and Rich waded to the shore and found a flat, grassy bank to rest. They ate a snack and adjusted their fishing lines.

"Another important concept to remember is asset allocation," Ernie said. "It's like having a range of flies to choose from to help you catch more fish.

"Asset allocation is simply diversifying your portfolio into various types of holdings. In the broadest sense it can be dividing among cash, fixed income, stocks, and alternative investments. Within most of these areas there are a multitude of sub-sets. As an example with stocks, there are big companies, mid-sized companies, and small companies. The investment folks call these large-cap, mid-cap, and small-cap. There are also growth and value stocks. The best example of a value stock is a company like General Electric. The quintessential growth stock is Apple. There are also domestic stocks and international stocks.

"Each of these has a place in a portfolio. Often, when one type of asset zigs, another type zags. The point is, you don't want to have all your eggs in one basket. Asset allocation is a way to lessen your risk and possibly even improve your returns."

Rich had heard of this concept of investing. "I used to work with a guy who had a saying: 'Early to bed, early to rise, diversify, diversify, diversify,'" Rich said.

"That's a good one. I'm going to remember that," Ernie said. "It's no wonder that you hear so much about this technique. Asset allocation and diversification are some of the only tools I know of that offer potentially higher returns with lower risk."

Ernie scanned the sky. There wasn't a cloud in sight. "I'm trying to remember the other couple of concepts my advisor walked me through when we revamped my plan a few years ago. One of them he called the mechanics of investing.

"The mechanics of investing is basically the nuts and bolts of putting your portfolio together. By this, I mean looking at the logistics of putting a portfolio together, and not necessarily the logistics and merits of selecting individual holdings. This gets a little technical, but I'm talking about studying the environment that you're investing in.

We start at the macro level, like looking at global gross domestic product forecasts and whether the global economy is expanding or contracting. Then we move to a more local level, looking at the U.S. and whether its economy is growing or slowing. Then we look at the markets themselves and how different markets are acting. For example, are the fixed-income and equity markets likely to increase or decrease in value based upon their current cycles?

"Within those markets, what about the subsets? Does growth offer more potential than value, or vice versa? Large, mid, or small—which looks best? International versus domestic?"

"You're starting to get over my head a bit," Rich said. "I didn't realize I was in for an economics class."

"Believe me, you'll get to know this stuff inside and out pretty quickly," Ernie said. "Imagine taking all that time and energy you used to spend at ACS and putting it into your investment plan, even just for a week. Investing some time up front will help you over the long run.

"When it comes to the mechanics of investing, you can work with your advisor to figure out which investment classes make sense based on opportunity and the risk you're willing to accept.

"That brings me to my next point," Ernie said. "You need trusted advice. Who are you going to work with now that Greg Webber isn't around to help?"

"Well, I'm not totally sure," Rich said. "After Greg died, his firm divided his clients among the other advisors in the office. I got a call from a young guy and we met once. He's a nice guy and he seems to know his stuff. I just wish Greg was around to help with this."

"You might ask the new guy for a reference, or figure out if you know anybody working with him," Ernie said. "A good financial advisor like Greg knows what he's doing and can easily cover his costs by keeping you on the right path and helping you stay away from trouble. You might take some time to figure out whether other folks have been comfortable with your new guy, or whether he's had any complaints against him.

"You just need someone good to help you out. You don't go to the cardiologist and tell him how to treat your old ticker. You need to trust him to help you," Ernie said.

"And speaking of old tickers, there are two more concepts that I try to keep in mind when it comes to investing. We're not going to be around forever, so make certain your estate is set up so that your heirs are taken care of after you're gone. By taking a hard look at your family, you will know if anything special is required. If Skip were to come into a lot of money, left to his own devices, I don't think it would last very long."

Ernie continued, "The second is you may live longer, or at least you'll probably be happier, if you understand the concept of news versus noise. My financial advisor has drilled this into me, especially during the turbulent markets of the past few years."

"What do you mean?" Rich said.

"Basically, I'm talking about tuning out all the hype and focusing on important news when it comes to investing," Ernie said.

"In today's news environment, there's always something to obsess over. Can you believe there was a time when investors looked at stock quotes once a day or less? The real-time reporting we get today doesn't necessarily lead to better investment decisions. The problem is that much of the breaking news really doesn't matter long-term to your investment portfolio. My advisor refers to this extra information as noise. There are very few things that have a true impact on long-term performance, and there's a lot of noise that causes short-term market volatility. Those fluctuations are often knee-jerk psychological reactions fueled by fear or greed.

"Don't get me wrong," Ernie said. "I love being able to look online or at the TV to get the latest market snapshot. Tom Keene on Bloomberg is nothing short of brilliant. And it's always fun to watch Maria Bartiromo on CNBC. But I have to remember not to panic. You can't let the news du jour throw you off your long-term plan. I recently learned this old expression: 'The market climbs a wall of worry.' In other words, there's always something to fret over and to worry about. That's one of the reasons I like to leave town for trips like these. It helps me step away from the noise."

"That makes a lot of sense," Richard said. "I've always tried to take market fluctuations with a grain of salt. But it can be hard. Greg was good at explaining the noise, as you call it."

"Speaking of noise, I think all this talk is scaring the fish," Ernie said. "I'm done talking and ready to fish."

Ernie and Rich ventured back into the stream for another couple hours of fishing. They covered about 200 yards, wandering up and down the stream looking for fish. Ernie caught six, while Rich pulled in a couple.

By about 6 p.m., Rich and Ernie were getting tired of fishing. They'd consumed their way through all of their crackers and cheese, and most of their water.

"You ready to head for the hotel?" Ernie said as he released another trout into the cold current.

"That's easy for you to say. You just caught one," Rich said.

"I'm not sure my stomach can wait for you to catch another fish," Ernie said. "This is a vacation, after all. I'm sure tomorrow will be your big day."

They gathered their equipment and scrambled up the bank to the Jeep. When they reached the road, Rich turned around to the scan the river and the forests rising up the opposite bank. It was always interesting to look back, from a higher view, on a river where you'd been fishing. It was like looking back on an experience from earlier in life, but with new perspective. Rich wondered how this transition would appear when he eventually looked back on it. He wanted to make the most of the opportunity.

Ernie's calm and confidence had made Rich feel better. Rich knew an investment plan was critical to his retirement, but it helped to hear it from Ernie. It was evident that Ernie had gotten his financial life in good order.

If Ernie could pull it off after three wives and too many girlfriends to recall—including Ernie's favorite, Brandy—then surely Rich and Peg could do it. The Vivas were spendthrift puritans compared to Ernie. "We can make this work," Rich thought, "and the investment plan provides a practical road map."

Ernie's cell phone buzzed as Rich drove back into town.

"Hello? Skip. . .is that you?" Ernie fell silent. "You can't be serious," he said. "Well, I'll start making some calls. Just don't do anything else stupid right now."

Rich looked at his friend. The color had drained from Ernie's face.

"What's the deal?" Rich said.

The call was from Ernie's 35-year-old son, Skip Troutman. He was calling from the Los Angeles County Jail, where he was nursing a hangover and facing charges of driving under the influence, disorderly conduct, cocaine possession, and violation of probation. Ernie took the news like a kick in his substantial belly. Skip's legal troubles had been a recurring issue over the past 10 years or so.

Ernie dialed his lawyer to start trying to get some help for Skip in California. Skip may have been a ne'er-do-well, but Ernie would always bail him out.

Rich thought about the history he knew of Skip. This episode sounded worse than his normal escapades. Ernie's strategy of throwing money at the problem had backfired repeatedly and it was an embarrassment to Ernie, especially considering his success and status.

Skip Troutman had moved to Los Angeles at the age of 25 to chase Hollywood glamour. He was a good-looking kid and he loved to party, but he never had any real concern for earning his way. Why should he? Dad was always there to bail him out. Skip's annual earnings paled in comparison to even one quarter of his dad's income from dividends.

Skip generally mooched off his girlfriends and his dad, who sent checks to assuage the guilt he felt over Skip's failures. Ernie had been somewhat of a wild man himself, but Ernie also relished making money, and he had found a way to channel his energy into business. Skip had inherited his father's love of the good life, but not his drive to pay for it. Ernie regretted it deeply—all those hours he had worked late, the all-nighters of feverish negotiations to forge the next big contract.

Ernie had overlooked Skip during the boy's formative years and tried to make up for it by buying him nice toys and pushing cash on him. Like many teens with lots of cash, Skip spent it on expensive hobbies like booze, marijuana, and cars. The problem was that he hadn't grown out of it. These days, it appeared, Skip was getting excitement from areas that would not be as forgiving.

Ernie often worried about what would happen to Skip once he was no longer around to bail him out. He was particularly concerned about all the trouble his son could get in with a windfall of inheritance—especially without anyone watching over him. As a result, Ernie set up trusts for Skip, to be funded upon Ernie's death. Ernie's ex-wife Roxanne, Skip's mother, would serve as trustee. If Roxanne was unable to serve, then a corporate trustee would take over.

To Rich, Ernie's heartache over his son was equally as enlightening as the financial lessons Ernie bestowed earlier in the day. While Ernie may have conquered his challenges in business and finances, he apparently mismanaged fatherhood and failed at raising a productive son with good financial sense. Why was it that so many truly talented and successful people tended to raise such irresponsible children?

Rich counted himself lucky in that regard. That was one area where he and Peg had excelled. Correct that: That was an area where Peg had excelled. She had raised two beautiful kids while Rich birthed and raised his own baby: ACS Inc.

Rich thought about his own family. His two children were quite different from one another. Laura, his 25-year-old daughter, was über-practical. She had studied chemical engineering at the University of Texas and secured a steady job before she even walked the graduation stage. No, Laura wasn't a major concern.

It was their son, 21-year-old Patrick, who Rich was more concerned about. Patrick was currently backpacking through Europe with his girlfriend, having dropped out of Louisiana State University to make the trip. And for reasons Rich couldn't fully explain, he and Peg were paying for the majority of their son's adventure. What made the Vivas' decision to pay for Patrick's dropout escapades across Europe any more excusable that Ernie continually paying off his son to ease his own guilt?

Ernie's situation with Skip made it obvious to Rich that he needed to talk with his son about money and work ethic. Maybe it was overreacting, but he thought about getting a call from Patrick like Ernie's call from Skip. Patrick needed to get his act together. What if Patrick viewed his father's business sale as a winning lottery ticket? It shouldn't be that way. Rich made a mental note to have a serious discussion with his son.

But Rich was conflicted. How could he make a convincing argument for his son to accept financial responsibility for his own life when Rich felt so confused about his own situation? He thought back to his conversation with Ernie about the investment plan.

Both Ernie's and Rich's financial advisors had emphasized the importance of starting an investment plan by setting goals and objectives. At the moment, Rich didn't know exactly what his goals were. For the first time, he had reached a point where he had time to really think about a meaningful plan that would cover the rest of his life. Several questions came to mind: "What if Peg and I live for four more decades? What about our kids? How do we offer Laura and Patrick a step up that we didn't have ourselves without turning them into another Skip? What about my legacy in the community?"

Rich could see why setting goals would be crucial to developing a financial plan that would provide a promising future for his family, hopefully for generations to come. He looked forward to discussing it with Peg, who always managed to elevate the discussion. It might actually be fun.

Rich pulled the Jeep into the parking lot at the Teton Village hotel. Ernie had been riding in silence after making several phone calls.

"You doing okay?" Rich asked.

"I could use a drink," Ernie said. "Let's stop by the bar before dinner. We could eat at the hotel restaurant, if you don't mind. Their breakfast this morning was pretty good."

"That sounds good," Rich responded. "Is there anything I can do to help with the Skip situation?"

"I've done what I can from here," Ernie said. "He probably deserves to go to jail, but I can't just watch it happen. My lawyer in Houston is calling his buddies in L.A. to deal with Skip. I'm thinking I might need to go there tomorrow."

Rich nodded. "I wouldn't blame you for that. I think that's what you need to do."

Ernie chuckled. "It's funny. All that talk today about planning. . .if only my family life were as stable as my financial plan."

Chapter 3

Goals, Planning, and National Parks

After Ernie's departure to Los Angeles, Rich had an extra day to himself in Jackson Hole before Peg flew in from Houston. Rich went into town for a bagel and coffee and to walk around the streets of Jackson. It was brisk and dry—a welcome relief from the Houston heat and humidity.

Rich strolled through the downtown square and watched tourists snapping photos under the arch of hundreds of elk antlers, an unusual entry gate made of antlers collected on the National Elk Refuge on the outskirts of town. In one western shop, a pair of intricately decorated cowboy boots caught his eye. He even tried them on, but decided against buying them. They felt stiff on his feet and looked ridiculous because he was wearing shorts.

After he'd walked most of the small downtown, Rich drove the rental Jeep south of town to once again try his hand at fly fishing. On his way, he dialed his daughter, Laura, to say hello.

It was mid-morning on a Friday, so Laura was probably tied up at her job at Exxon Mobil Corp. in Houston. Laura was 25 and had been working as a chemical engineer at Exxon for one year. She was a smart young woman. Despite her father's advice to go to Texas A&M, she'd attended the University of Texas at Austin to pursue a biology degree, and followed that with a master's degree in chemical engineering. She had no problem finding a job upon graduation.

Laura's cell phone went to voice mail, so Rich left a short message saying hello "from the splendor of Jackson Hole." Rich thought about all the times he'd been busy in meetings or on the job site and unable to answer family phone calls. The tables had turned. Now that he finally had spare time on a workday morning, Laura was just beginning her career. She would be too busy to chat during workdays for decades to come, probably for the rest of Rich's life.

Rich steered the Jeep onto a pullout alongside Snake River. He put on his rented fishing boots and waders, and grabbed his vest and rod. Ernie had told him that midday wasn't necessarily the best time to catch trout, but it didn't really matter to Rich. It sure was pleasant outside. The weather was cool, with a hint of pending fall in the breeze. The aspen and cottonwood trees were blazing yellow.

Rich dropped his fly into an eddy behind a river stone to test his luck. Nothing. After a few minutes, he waded carefully upstream a dozen yards to another spot and tried again. Still no bites. So Rich reeled in his line and changed the fly. It should have been a simple task, but it took him 10 minutes.

Rich thought back to the day before and his fishing venture with Ernie. They'd had a terrific day, at least until Skip's jailhouse phone call. Ernie had talked about the importance of asset allocation and diversifying an investment portfolio. He wondered if his small collection of flies could be compared to asset allocation. If the trout didn't like one fly, he could always try another. In the same way, if one section of his portfolio wasn't performing, such as small-cap stocks, he could hopefully count on another to produce returns.

But what if the fish were already full on real bugs, or if there just weren't any fish in the river? Then it wouldn't matter what kind of fly he used. He still wouldn't catch anything. This had been one of Rich's long-standing concerns about investing, and it had taken on new importance now that he was retired. What if the economy was shrinking and everything was losing value? Like fishing a river with no fish, would it even matter if he had a diversified investment portfolio? Would anything produce returns for him and Peg to live on?

Rich felt a tug on his line. He popped the rod up to set the hook and pulled in the line. He saw the trout with the line it its mouth, twisting in the current. Rich pulled up the fish, grabbed hold of its body, and carefully threaded the hook out of its mouth. It was a small rainbow trout. He admired the fish for a moment. Lines of translucent color striped the length of its silvery body. He dropped the fish in the water, and it immediately darted downstream to another pool.

Catching the fish settled Rich's mind. He considered himself an incompetent fisherman, but he had made the effort and caught a fish. In the same way, he hoped he would reap the possible rewards of investing by making the effort.

The little rainbow trout turned out to be the most exciting part of Rich's fishing day. After another hour or so of wading to different points in the river, he had not replicated his success. He saw the fun and relaxation in fishing, but it didn't hold his attention when he didn't have a friend along to share the experience. Ernie, not the fishing, had been his primary entertainment the day before.

Rich gathered his gear and trudged back to the Jeep. He stopped in town for a buffalo burger on his way to the hotel. By mid-afternoon, Rich was content to lounge around the hotel. He hiked the grounds, watched bad daytime TV shows he had never seen before, and bought a few magazines at the gift shop that he hadn't had the time to read in years.

Peg's flight arrived the following morning. Rich checked out of his hotel and drove through the valley to the airport to meet her arriving flight.

Peg was obviously excited as she walked briskly into the terminal, pulling her rolling bag. She wore her hiking boots and sun hat, ready for the outdoors.

"That was an amazing landing," she said. "It was so beautiful to descend into the valley and see the mountains and forests. I can't wait to get out there and see the country."

Rich hugged Peg and took her bag.

"You look relaxed," Peg said.

"I'm feeling pretty relaxed," Rich responded. "I've basically been hanging out for a couple of days. I've been fishing for two days in a row and I've been eating good at every meal. Can you believe I even watched TV and read magazines?"

Peg's eyebrows arched. "So Mr. Workaholic finds there could be other things to think about than air compression? I was hoping this day would come."

"There's a lot to think about, that's for sure," Rich said. "But we'll have plenty of time for that. You've got to see the Jeep I rented. Are you ready to head to the park?"

"Definitely."

The Vivas had reservations at the Jenny Lake Lodge in Grand Teton National Park. The pair had talked for years about an autumn trip to Grand Teton and Yellowstone to escape the Texas Indian summer, but there was always a catch. Work interfered, or they ended up traveling elsewhere with family and friends.

As they drove through the valley to the park entrance, the stone-gray clouds that had gathered over the Tetons dropped a short, intense burst of rain. The downpour was such that Rich pulled over for a couple of minutes because the Jeep's windshield wipers couldn't keep up with the deluge. He had rarely taken such a precaution in the past.

Rich was looking forward to talking about investment plans with his wife. He wanted her help on the project. Peg was financially savvy, and he'd found that it was always better to get her input on the front end.

"Have you heard anything from Ernie?" Peg asked as they sat and listened to the rain in the shelter of the vehicle.

"No. I suspect he's had his hands full dealing with lawyers in Los Angeles."

Peg shook her head. "That is really sad. I guess he's somewhat used to it by now, but I just can't imagine the stress."

"Ernie's a relaxed guy, but he was pretty shaken when Skip called from jail. I felt bad because we were having a good time up until he got the call. We did some good fishing and Ernie was giving me his two cents on investing."

"That's good," Peg remarked. "Ernie seems to know how to handle his money."

"I think so," Rich said. The rain had let up and he pulled the Jeep back onto the road.

"He gave me some interesting things to think about. I'm hoping we'll get a chance to talk about our financial situation some on this trip."

"Okay."

They were driving through vast pastures staked by wooden fences. The cattle had taken shelter under cottonwood trees during the storm. The sun had reappeared, and its rays were bouncing brightly off the wet surface of the grass.

They approached the park entrance.

"But we'll have plenty of time for that," Rich said. "I want to give you some time to soak in the splendor here and unwind from the city."

Peg giggled at her husband's uncharacteristic remark. "I could get used to this laid-back side of yours."

The Jenny Lake Lodge was a collection of rustic but luxurious cabins set in a scenic valley under the shadow of the Tetons.

They checked in to their cabin and unpacked. Back at the lobby, Peg had come across a flyer for an educational talk at the visitor center taking place in 30 minutes. They decided to check it out.

The center's floor-to-ceiling windows provided a magnificent view of the Tetons. By then, the sky was intensely blue again. The sun was starting to shift toward the mountains and cast a golden glow over the valley. The wind had blown away any sign of clouds or rain. In the center's main room, a few rows of folding chairs were lined up facing a podium.

The speaker for the evening's presentation was Sally Victor. Her talk was titled "Forest Management: Different Goals, Different Strategies."

"I walked away from corporate America and millions of dollars to study this stuff, so I hope you'll pay attention," Sally quipped to start things off.

The small audience laughed at Sally's remark. She had quickly taken command of the room.

Sally was a petite woman, probably in her late 60s or 70s, with short gray hair. She introduced herself as a forester from Colorado who occasionally volunteered at national parks as a guide and lecturer.

Rich liked Sally's comfortable and confident style; she looked like she would be at home in front of a corporate board room.

Sally said her presentation would focus on forest management and the different ways that the National Park Service, the U.S. Forest Service, and private timber companies manage their lands.

"The government set the national parks aside, like this one, to last an eternity," Sally said. "But the natural world can't be sealed off and protected like a museum exhibit."

National parks, such as Yellowstone and Grand Teton, are tightly focused on preserving the pristine natural state of the land and its plants and animals, Sally explained. Still, natural occurrences occur that threaten the park's ecosystem. Think of blister rust and beetle outbreaks that kill off large swaths of trees in the forest.

"So managers of these parks turn to a tool that's been around since before we humans ever interfered," Sally said. "It's called fire."

In the past, the parks would suppress fires, but they eventually realized they were causing more harm than good. Under the natural fire management plans they use today, park managers generally allow naturally occurring fires—those started by lightning strikes—to take their course.

"The fires rejuvenate the forest by burning out aged trees and depositing ash and nutrients that regenerate growth of plants," Sally said.

"There's no question that fire carries risks," Sally said. "There are many examples of fires going out of control to a dangerous degree. That includes the infamous Yellowstone fires that burned up much of the park, just up the road from here, in 1988. Still, fires are the most natural land management tool that we have."

Sally moved on to national forests.

"We're in a national park, but a lot of the land around the park is national forest land," she said. "There are more than 190 million acres of national forest in the United States, which is about 9 percent of the country."

The U.S. Forest Service calls its land "the land of many uses." It works to protect the forest while also allowing multiple uses—

everything from snow skiing to elk hunting, cattle ranching, gold mining, and logging.

"The Forest Service's management challenge is to balance appropriate economic development activity while also protecting the forest's basic value as natural environment," Sally explained.

The Forest Service has land-management tools such as controlled fires, or allowing logging or cattle grazing on certain lands.

"But for the Forest Service, its tools really boil down to policy decisions," Sally said. "They must decide what to allow as far as the extent and location of human-caused disturbances to the natural environment."

Sally explained that the Teddy Roosevelt administration had established the Forest Service as a division of the Department of Agriculture in the early 1900s.

"Would he even recognize the Forest Service today, with its annual budget of about $6 billion and more than 34,000 employees?" she asked. "Over the years, Congress has modified the mandate of the Forest Service as needed, but I think Teddy would be proud of its motto: 'Caring for the land and serving people.'

"It's a tough balancing act. If any of you live near a national forest, you've probably heard plenty of bickering about grazing, motocross bikes, oil and gas drilling, and so on."

Having completed her description of national park and national forest land management, Sally turned her attention to timber companies and their approach to land management.

"Timber companies manage their property with the goal of maximizing use and harvesting profits," Sally explained. "They grow as many pulp trees as possible."

Timber companies routinely harvest the trees from their property and then replant. They harvest and plant in a rotation across the property, which means they always have trees at different stages of development. The younger trees require minimum treatment because they tend to be resistant to insects and diseases.

"As the trees get older and require more attention, it's time to harvest them and make some money," Sally said.

Sally wrapped up her presentation and fielded a few questions. The whole thing was over in an efficient 45 minutes. The Vivas spent a few minutes touring the visitor center to learn more about the park. It was getting late, so they decided to head back to the lodge.

Rich had enjoyed Sally's talk. The natural beauty of the park was actually the product of tremendous thought and planning. He understood why people valued the pristine land. Over the course of a few days, the stunning beauty of the vast mountains, valleys, and rivers had helped relieve his mind from its preoccupation with the business sale and investment planning. He thought about John D. Rockefeller Jr. and his mission to buy much of the land in the Jackson Hole area so the government could preserve it for future generations.

Rich drove slowly through a forested area of the park, while Peg watched the forest for any sign of moose, bears, or elk.

"I don't see us funding any national treasures, but I hope we can find a way to contribute to future generations of Vivas," Rich said.

"What are you talking about?" Peg asked, her wildlife concentration broken.

"Wouldn't it be great to know that if we invest wisely we could leave an inheritance to our children and our children's children?"

Peg smiled. She was hoping the visit to the national parks would help relieve Rich's anxiety and give him some perspective on their life situation.

"Of course! There's no reason we can't do that."

"I was impressed with Sally Victor's forest management talk," Peg added. "The way these ecosystems work in harmony is really inspiring. Sally struck me as a wise woman. I'd be curious to learn more about her."

The Vivas didn't have to wait long to meet Sally Victor. The next morning, she was seated at a neighboring table in the lodge's dining room.

Sally was having breakfast with her grandson, Justin. As the meal wound down, Peg took the chance to introduce herself and Rich to Sally. They complimented Sally on her forestry presentation. Sally was very gracious, and after a short conversation, she invited the Vivas to join her table for coffee.

Sally said she and Justin were visiting the park to celebrate his recent graduation from the University of Colorado with a degree in environmental science.

"But this poor boy must think I invited him here to torture him with business talk," Sally laughed.

Justin shrugged his shoulders and smiled. "I don't mind. I figure it's important stuff."

"At least he's gracious about listening to me," Sally said.

"Trusted advice is always good," Rich said. "As for me, I've been trying to steer clear of too much business talk, but it can be tough to leave it behind."

"I know what you mean," Sally responded. "I've been retired from business for 25 years, but money and investing and finance still always seem to be on my mind."

"So you really did walk away from corporate America like you mentioned in your talk the other day?" Richard asked.

"Oh, yes," Sally said. "And I never looked back."

She shared her story as the four of them sat together, drinking coffee and looking out over the beautiful meadow with the Grand Tetons in the distance.

Sally had once been an executive at a major Wall Street firm, making $100 million handshake deals over power lunches. But at the age of 50, at the pinnacle of her career, the stress and hours of her job started to drag her down.

She had earned plenty of money by that point, and her husband had always wanted to move out West. So she decided to walk away from her finance job and go back to school to get her master's degree in wildlife ecology from Colorado State University.

It was a big change for a formidable businesswoman, but once she made the shift, she was happy with her decision. She knew the business world like few others, but she was equally interested in and passionate about the natural world, especially the Rockies.

"Now I'm trying to give Justin some investment advice," Sally said, "but I keep finding myself putting it in terms we both enjoy more: nature and the environment."

"What do you mean?" Richard asked.

"Well, let's take yesterday's talk," Sally said. "I focused on different management policies for national parks, national forests, and timber companies. Each group manages its land to reach its specific goals. How is that different from three investors making portfolio decisions to meet their specific goals? Or there could be one investor who's trying to meet multiple goals. It's all about setting your goals and developing a plan to reach them."

"I knew there was more to you than hiking boots and a sun hat," Peg said.

"I think I blend in pretty well," Sally said, smiling.

She continued her explanation.

"Like I said yesterday, national parks are meant to last an eternity," Sally said.

National park managers take a conservative approach, just like an investor who wants to protect his or her capital.

"That would be someone like me," Sally said. "At my age, I don't want to take risks with my portfolio. I want it to withstand the test of time for me and my heirs, just like a national park."

"What about the fires?" Peg asked. "I remember you saying national parks allow fires to help maintain the health of the forest."

Sally mulled it over.

"It's a good question," she said. "You certainly don't want to burn your portfolio. I think I see the fires as a representation of a riskier investment within a predominantly conservative portfolio."

Any investment plan will run into problems, with or without the inclusion of some risk. In forest terms, those problems might be tree diseases or bark beetles. Fires help burn out old and decaying parts of the forest, giving the forest new life. In the same way, a small amount of risk, and the potential return it generates, can help offset unforeseen portfolio problems and give the portfolio vitality.

"Many investors think of risk simply as volatility of performance. However, the risk of outliving your money is equally if not more important in my book!" Sally said, her voice rising along with her eyebrows. "You want to preserve your nest egg, but you don't want to outlive it."

"Now, you'll remember I talked about national forests as well. They're a different story."

National forests are working to balance multiple uses like hunting, mining, logging, and ranching, while also preserving the forest's environmental integrity.

"The Forest Service wants to provide space for economic activity, but not to the point that it destroys the forest," Sally said. "I would compare their management to an active portfolio that's meant to provide moderate income while also preserving the investor's basic assets."

Rich shook his head. "I don't get it."

"This might best be compared to a situation like yours," Sally explained. "I see the Forest Service approach like an investment portfolio that's meant to allow for growth and cash flow, but it should also safely provide for the investor over his lifetime."

"I think I see it," Peg remarked. "It's like the middle road between growth and preservation."

"Right," Sally responded. "So, the final example is the timber companies. They represent a more aggressive approach. The timber company management style would be comparable to managing a portfolio for someone Justin's age. The timber company has one major goal, and that is to make money."

Timber companies are constantly investing in new seedlings and harvesting. It's an active and risk-prone management policy aimed at making money. They plant in a rotation, so there's always a fresh crop of mature trees ready for harvest.

"Without hedges, it's risky, because what if the timber market falls?" Sally said. "But it can also be very lucrative, because you're constantly harvesting gains when housing starts are up and the timber market is hot."

Hedging is a strategy of locking in a set price for something that you're going to buy or sell in the future.

"So if you're a young person like Justin, that's the better investment approach," Sally said. "Why not take the risk and chase hot stocks—within reason, of course—because you'll have time to rebuild if an investment doesn't work?

"Sometimes timber companies hold off on harvesting trees when they feel timber is undervalued. Similar to a young investor, who has time on his side, the timber companies have a long time horizon, because it can take 20 years or more before timber is ready for harvest. These days, timber companies often diversify their income by allowing activities such as hunting on their land."

Sally took a sip of her coffee and peered out the window at a bald eagle perched on a cottonwood branch.

"That brings up another point about all this. It's not like we're all going different directions in investing, or in forest management," Sally said. "There are definitely similarities."

"I wondered about that," Peg responded. "I was thinking it's probably good to have an element of risk in everyone's portfolio, regardless of age."

Sally nodded her head. "Indeed. Even an old person like me has some room for a timber company approach, though I think of myself as more of a national park gal."

The Park Service, Forest Service, and timber companies must all be good stewards of the land or they won't be viable, Sally added. Also, the landscape as a whole benefits from the good graces of Mother Nature when she delivers the right mix of rain, sun, and temperature.

"I guess that would be like a good day at the market," Rich said.

"I agree," Sally answered. "On days when the market grows, most of us benefit. Justin may benefit more than us, because his portfolio may jump the most, but we all benefit. It's helpful to look to outside analogies, but I believe it's fair to say that all of us would like to see our net worths larger.

"The important part is to find your primary goals and to align a strategy that has the potential to meet those goals," Sally said. "You see, just like in forest management, different goals dictate different strategies."

"Wow," Rich said. "I think you're onto something."

Sally smiled and drank the last sip of her coffee. "I could go on, I suppose, but then I'd have to bill you."

Chapter 4

Goals and Objectives

Rich and Peg spent the next four days sightseeing around Grand Teton and Yellowstone National Parks. They hiked the trails, rented bikes for an excursion, and even took a rafting trip down the Snake River. The days were warm and bright; the nights were chilly. The Vivas saw eagles, elk, moose, and bears during their drives and hikes through the parks. They ate nice meals at the lodge and in town at Jackson restaurants. In the evenings, they soaked their bones in the lodge hot tub. It was one of the most relaxing vacations they'd ever taken.

Rich had mostly steered clear of financial planning since their discussion with Sally Victor. With days full of quiet time, however, the topic crept into his mind from time to time. A recurring theme had developed during his recent discussions about retirement planning. In his talks with Ernie and Sally, as well as the young financial advisor he spoke with after Greg Webber died, each had mentioned the importance of an investor's goals and objectives.

The advisor had asked Rich about his goals for money and lifestyle planning. Rich had given it some thought, but hadn't settled on any specifics. Then, Ernie had explained the vital importance of goals and objectives in the development of a financial plan. And in Sally's discussion of forest management, she had made it clear that an investor's goals and objectives were the primary factors in developing an investment strategy. The only way for Rich to achieve his goals would be to first identify where he wanted to go. This actually made a great deal of sense to Rich, who had been goal-oriented for his entire life—especially in business.

On the final morning of their trip, Rich and Peg packed their bags and then stopped at the lodge dining room for breakfast. They took their time, enjoying the view of the yellowing cottonwoods in the meadow and the Teton peaks gleaming in the intense morning sun.

"I'm going to miss this place," Peg said. "It's hard to imagine people actually live here and get to see this every day."

"Me too," Rich said. "But don't forget about the winters—frigid and snowy from what I hear."

"I think it would be worth it," Peg responded. "The good news is that even though we live in Houston, we now have the time and money to visit places like this more often."

"Let's hope so," Rich said. "I know we've got the time these days, but I don't know about the money."

Peg sighed with a slight smile. She didn't know if her husband would ever feel like he was wealthy, even though he was a multimillionaire. That was probably a good thing, she thought, as long as he didn't turn into a nervous miser.

Rich's apprehension wasn't uncommon. Rarely do people feel like they're wealthy, even when by all standards they are.

"That's what confuses me about retirement," Rich said. "Now we've got all this time to do fun things, but we no longer have steady income to pay for it."

"That's what a financial plan is all about," Peg said. "We can make an investment strategy that will help us meet our goals, such as yearly—no, twice-yearly—trips to Jackson Hole."

Rich smiled at his wife's enthusiasm. She was always getting caught up in the moment. But she'd also hit on that recurring theme again.

"You mentioned goals," Rich said. "I've been thinking about recent conversations with Sally Victor, Ernie, and the financial advisor. It seems like our next step, or first step, should be to set our goals."

"That makes sense to me," Peg said.

"To do that, we need to figure out exactly how much cash we need each month to live on, and then how much we need for all the vacations you're planning," Rich said.

"That sounds like a good project for the airplane," Peg said. "I don't want to think about monthly spending during our final moments here at Grand Teton."

"Fair enough," Rich said.

They finished breakfast, loaded their bags into the Jeep, and set off for the Jackson Hole airport.

The flight was on schedule. Rich and Peg boarded the plane and settled into their seats. Rich grabbed a notebook and pen from his bag and wrote "GOALS & OBJECTIVES" at the top of a page.

"So is it possible to say how much money we spend on a regular basis, every month?" Rich asked Peg.

He figured the first goal would be to make sure they had enough money to live on.

Peg put down the new copy of *People* she had purchased in the airport and rolled her eyes.

"I'm still in vacation mode, not worry-about-money mode," Peg said.

But Rich needed her help and input. Not only were their goals a shared pursuit, Peg was also the bookkeeper for their household. Peg had always paid the bills because Rich was too busy with Apex Compression Services.

"Oh, come on. This is planning—one of your favorite activities," Rich said.

That elicited a laugh from Peg, who closed the magazine and looked over at Rich's notebook.

Rich continued, "To set our goals and objectives, we need to figure out exactly how much cash we need each month. So how much do we spend on all our bills—utilities and whatever else?"

"That's hard to say exactly," Peg responded. "I don't think we need to get down to the penny, because there will always be some differences from month to month, like if we go on vacation, donate to a charity, or buy a new TV or dishwasher."

"Then let's shoot for an estimate," Rich said.

Peg thought about their monthly credit card bill, which covered almost all of their monthly expenses. There were grocery bills, restaurant tabs, utilities, cable service, country club fees, mortgage payments, and monthly contributions to their church.

"It normally works out to about $20,000 a month," Peg said.

Rich arched his eyebrows in disbelief. "Wow, that can't be right."

"What, you think you're still in college?" Peg said. "We've got a nice lifestyle, thanks to your hard work, and it costs money."

With a base spending level of about $20,000 a month, the Vivas agreed that they should budget $250,000 per year for living expenses.

"But now we've got even more time to spend money," Rich said. "I wonder if we will end up spending more than we did before we sold the company?"

"Well, we can always downsize and reduce spending, but I think you raise a good point. Since we're talking goals and objectives, we should probably consider an ideal scenario and aim for that."

"How about $300,000 per year, then?" Rich asked, still incredulous that they could spend that much.

Peg nodded in agreement.

Rich put pen to paper and wrote: "Goal One: Cash flow of $300,000 per year."

"Okay," Peg said. "Now let's think about goals more exciting than monthly expenses."

Rich thought back to his conversations with the financial advisor and Ernie.

"Now that we have cash flow and our living expenses covered, our goals and objectives are also supposed to encompass our approach to saving and investing. For example, how conservative or aggressive do we want to be with our investments?"

One of the questions the Vivas needed to consider was whether they already had enough money, whether they wanted to take some risk to make more money, or whether they wanted to take a conservative, protective approach?

Their net worth was about $16 million, including the $12 million profit from the sale of ACS. Rich figured he was like everybody else: He wanted to protect his money and grow it. Most of all, though, he definitely didn't want to lose what they had worked so hard to build.

"I agree with that," Peg said. "It sounds like our primary investment goal is to protect our money, but we also want to use it to make more money. After all, we should be good stewards of what we are fortunate to have."

They understood that accepting risk was part of investing, but they didn't want to lose their money and start from scratch. Being in their late 50s, they didn't have a lifetime to rebuild their savings if their investments washed out.

Rich recorded the goal in the notebook. "Goal Two: We made the money and we want it to grow, but we don't want to lose it. We want moderate growth, and we want to make sure to protect what we started with. We are willing to take some risk, but not high levels of risk."

Rich stopped for a moment and thought about his second goal. He had worked awfully hard to earn his money, and he had enjoyed the challenge. Wasn't it now time to reap the rewards and enjoy life?

"I don't want this to be super-stressful," he remarked.

"What do you mean?" Peg said.

"I mean investing. We didn't sell the company to become full-time investors. I don't want these investments to dominate our life."

"That should definitely be a goal," Peg said. "I think it fits really well with what we're trying to do in setting these goals. We need to find someone we trust to help manage our investments so that it's not a constant pain in the neck." (See Exhibit 4.1.)

Peg took the notebook and set it on her lap. She recorded the third goal.

"Goal Three: Make an investment strategy that we're comfortable with and doesn't stress us out. Develop a good relationship with a financial advisor. Allow the financial advisor to deflect the anxiety of investing. Don't worry about our money all the time."

"It seems like you've given that one some thought," Rich said.

S&P 500 Index Total Returns from 1937 to 2011

Less than (20%)	(20%) to (12%)	(12%) to (8%)	(8%) to 0	0 to 8%	8% to 12%	12% to 20%	More than 20%
1937 −33.93%	1973 −14.50%	1940 −9.71%	1939 −0.46%	1947 5.49%	1959 11.79%	1942 19.22%	1938 29.38%
1974 −26.03%		1941 −11.15%	1953 −1.17%	1948 5.42%	1968 10.84%	1944 19.28%	1943 25.69%
2002 −21.97%		1946 −7.78%	1977 −7.16%	1956 6.44%	1993 9.92%	1952 17.71%	1945 35.69%
2008 −36.55%		1957 −10.48%	1981 −4.85%	1960 0.28%	2004 10.74%	1964 16.30%	1949 22.30%
		1962 −8.83%	1990 −3.13%	1970 3.33%		1965 12.27%	1950 31.45%
		1966 −9.99%		1978 6.39%		1971 14.15%	1951 23.25%
		1969 −8.32%		1984 5.97%		1972 18.88%	1954 51.23%
		2000 −9.03%		1987 5.67%		1979 18.18%	1955 30.96%
		2001 −11.85%		1992 7.43%		1986 18.54%	1958 42.44%
				1994 1.28%		1988 16.35%	1961 26.61%
				2005 4.83%		2006 15.61%	1963 22.50%
				2007 5.48%		2010 14.82%	1967 23.72%
				2011 2.10%			1975 36.92%
							1976 23.64%
							1980 31.52%
							1982 20.37%
							1983 22.31%
							1985 31.05%
							1989 31.22%
							1991 30.00%
							1995 37.12%
							1996 22.68%
							1997 33.10%
							1998 28.34%
							1999 20.89%
							2003 28.36%
							2009 25.94%

8% to 12%

1959	11.79%
1968	10.84%
1993	9.92%
2004	10.74%

Data source: Bloomberg and Standard & Poor's
Data before 1957 are based on S&P 500 predecessor indices

Exhibit 4.1 For the last 75 years the S&P 500 (and predecessor S&P indices) has averaged a 9.88 percent annualized total return, yet there are only four instances where the S&P returned between 2 percent above or below the 75-year annual average return. This level of volatility can be challenging without knowing the historical nature of volatility in the equity markets.

"Not really," Peg responded. "It's just the whole idea of hiring someone to do it and not stressing all the time. Remember a few years ago, when you tried to repave the driveway and concrete spilled halfway across the lawn? You got really upset and it ended up costing about four times what it would have if we had just hired someone to do it in the first place."

"Don't remind me," Rich said, smiling at the absurdity of that regrettable situation.

"That's what I'm talking about here," Peg said.

"Okay. We're on the same page," Rich answered. "Now what about other goals? One thing the financial advisor mentioned was a vacation home. I've always liked the idea, but it never seemed very practical. Now that I'm not working all the time, it's easier to envision. What do you think?"

"That's hard for me to fathom," Peg said. "We have a hard enough time keeping up our own home, much less a second home. There are too many places I want to go for me to want to commit all my time to a specific vacation spot. But I sure would love to have a home in the mountains. Could we even afford that over the long term?"

"I don't know, but we may as well think big," Rich said. "We've got time to figure it out."

They talked about their options. Being Texans, it was hard to not fantasize about owning a ranch, maybe in the Hill Country or near Rich's hometown of Bryan.

"The ranch idea sounds good," Peg said. "The only thing I'd worry about is the work involved. We'd have to make sure we could afford a caretaker of some kind."

"That's true," Rich said. "We're talking about a vacation spot, not becoming full-time ranchers."

They also discussed one of their favorite vacation destinations, Scenic Highway 30A in Florida between Rosemary Beach and Grayton Beach. With sand as white as snow and water a mix of aqua blues and emerald green, they always found relaxation when they visited. The laid-back lifestyle of going virtually everywhere by bicycle took them to a less-complicated place, away from the hustle and bustle of the big city.

Of course, in an effort to escape the Texas heat they had always enjoyed their brief jaunts to the mountains during the summers. The two weeks in Jackson Hole had confirmed their belief that they could fit in easily with the mountain lifestyle.

"Jackson Hole is heaven on earth but it's not the easiest place to get in and out of," said Peg, always practical. "There's no direct flight from Houston and it is too far of a drive."

"It sure would be nice," Rich said. "It's pretty far from Houston, though. Maybe I could finally conquer fly fishing."

Rich immediately found himself in his Type A work mode, thinking to himself that if he could somehow double their net worth, then perhaps they could have access to a private jet that would make it a snap to fly to Jackson Hole. Isn't it interesting that, regardless of one's net worth, there's almost always something bigger and better? After he thought it over for a minute, he quickly came to the conclusion that he did not want to take any huge bet to get to the next level, nor did he want to start over. He remembered goal number two; a moderate and steady approach would serve them well.

"What about a place in Colorado?" Rich asked.

Beaver Creek and Vail had long been other favorite quick destinations during the few getaways Rich and Peg had taken over the years.

"It's an easy flight to Denver from Houston, and the drive from Denver isn't bad," Peg said. "In the winter there's a direct into Eagle Vail. Besides, now that we have more time, we could drive up for the summer and bring the dogs."

"That settles it," Richard said. "One day we should have a place in the mountains of Colorado and if that goes well, perhaps we will consider a place on the beach along 30A in Florida."

Peg grinned. "Rich Viva, that's what I love about you: You're a big dreamer but somehow you seem to make these dreams a reality. I'm along for the ride, Rich. You haven't let me down yet."

"Maybe this retirement and goal setting can work hand in hand," Rich thought. He had set goals throughout his business career and it made total sense that he would use it for his financial future, as well.

Rich took the notebook and wrote down the fourth goal: "Buy a vacation home, maybe even two. Not sure if we want the extra responsibility, but let's decide within the next couple of years."

Rich marveled at the possibilities. What an improbable concept compared to his boyhood days of a rare Galveston trip with his family. But this was a new era. They had money and time. He didn't want to write off the idea completely. Maybe it wouldn't be a vacation home, but it could be another big expense like a sailboat or an RV.

Then there was the idea of legacy. At 58, Rich felt healthy and active. He wasn't knocking on heaven's door, but he also accepted that he was on the downhill side of life's mountain.

"What about the kids?" Rich asked. "We've always said that we'd like to leave an inheritance to them. Do you think we should make that one of our 'official' goals? And while we're at it, an inheritance for the next generation after them, if Pat and Laura ever have any kids?"

They talked about Patrick, probably drinking wine in a French cafe right about then. It upset Peg that he had dropped out of college. Rich thought it was immature. They both wanted their children to experience the world, but hated to see their son putting off reality.

"I want to help the kids, but I don't want to disincentivize their work ethic," Rich said. "There should be a way to leave them a sensible amount. I have a hard time believing there would be so much money left over that they could get away without working themselves."

Even with a net worth of $16 million, the Vivas needed to plan for at least three more decades of living expenses. And when it came to inheritance, much of the remainder could be lost to estate taxes if they didn't plan appropriately.

"I think our goal should be to enjoy our money while we can, and also to leave money to the kids," Peg said. "With $16 million, we should be able to do this and whatever else comes to mind."

Rich shook his head. "Let's not get carried away," he said. "Since the time we've boarded this plane, we're up to a house in Houston, another in the Colorado mountains, and a third along the Florida Gulf coast. We may be asking the kids for a loan!"

"You're the dreamer, Rich, so dream a little," Peg said. "We can work out whether the logic and the numbers support this later."

"Speaking of the kids, I would love nothing more than to see both of them happily married with children of their own," Peg continued. "If I could somehow will these late-bloomer children of ours into get married and having kids that would be great. But I'm not counting on it just yet."

"In due time," Rich said. "There's no sense getting worked up over that because it's well beyond our control. Chances are, they'll both have children. I'd like to be able to help those little ones as well, if possible."

"That would be wonderful," Peg said. "In fact, one day I looked into opening 529 plans for our future grandchildren, until I ran into a problem."

A 529 plan is named after a section of the IRS code that allows one to place money in a state-affiliated investment vehicle that grows tax free if used for higher educational expenses.

"What was the problem?" Rich asked.

"You can't establish that type of account for someone who isn't alive yet," Peg said. "These future grandkids need to be here with social security numbers before we can do that. But you know, it doesn't preclude us from earmarking part of our portfolio toward one day funding 529 plans for those eventual grandbabies."

Rich wrote down the fifth goal: "Provide money for the kids and grandkids. Come up with something that makes sense for the next three decades or longer—for us and for an inheritance for our kids, and someday, grandkids."

The topics of money and the kids got Rich thinking. Maybe he should make a goal of trying to teach some financial sense to the children? Having just sold a business and now living off of savings and investments, Rich thought it would definitely behoove Patrick and Laura to learn about stretching the family assets to their greatest advantage. He recalled hearing the pastor at their church say that the best investment is one in people, not just your portfolio. He couldn't help but wonder if he had made a big enough investment in the kids over the years. Before he had a chance to voice this, Peg was one step ahead.

Peg liked the idea of investing in future generations. "I absolutely want to take care of them, but we've already given them a lot," she said. "More money should mean more responsibility for them."

"Yes," Rich said. "I don't want to end up in the same situation as Ernie, feeding money to his addict son and then paying to try to clean up the mess."

"Well, I think we're in the clear with Laura," Peg said. "She's got her head screwed on pretty straight. But I still wonder about Patrick."

Peg took the notebook and wrote, "Goal Six: Talk with the kids about money and try to help them learn good money sense."

For the first time, Rich realized it might be easier to leave a financial inheritance or give money to his two kids than to teach them about the importance of managing their money.

"What else?" Peg asked.

Rich looked up the aisle and watched a toddler trying to break free from his parents and run toward the drink cart. He remembered why he and Peg limited their plane travel when they were young parents.

"The only other thing that comes to mind is the church," Rich said.

The Vivas had been members of Grace Methodist Church since the children were born. They had joined in the interest of developing a good community of friends for themselves and their children. Over the years, Grace Methodist had provided much more for them.

"I've always admired it when folks leave something to the church foundation when they pass on," Rich said. "Like when old Henry Johnson died. His will left enough to the church foundation that it has probably generated thousands of dollars over the course of a few years.

"That's thousands of dollars to offer scholarships for kids wanting to go to college, and other worthwhile projects like mosquito nets in Africa, along with the hospitals and libraries being established there," Rich said.

Peg added, "If we do this right, there's no reason we can't help our own future grandkids get a great education and also leave enough for other kids to do the same through the church foundation.

"Now that we're no longer donating from income, we should think about trying to build annual donations into our financial plan,"

Peg said. "It would be fun to see all of the good this money could do while we are alive and here to enjoy it."

Peg was also active in the Founders Club at Houston TUTS— Theatre Under The Stars. She mentioned that maybe she'd like to leave money to that group as well. And then there was the Interfaith Soup Kitchen, where they both volunteered during the holiday season each year. There was no shortage of worthy causes and charities to choose from.

"We won't know until we put pencil to paper what we can afford in this regard, but I think it's a worthy goal," Rich said.

He wrote, "Goal Seven: Provide money for the church foundation, and possibly charities."

"I think that's enough for now," Rich said. He thought back to his annual New Year's resolutions lists. The longer the lists, the less likely he was to meet his goals.

"It's a neat exercise," Peg said. "I always love planning and goal-setting, but this is definitely a unique set of goals for us."

"It's true," Rich responded. "I figure we can make changes to this list now that we're in the mind frame of thinking about it. This gives us a good start and something to bring to the table when we meet with the financial advisor. I think we're on the right track."

The Vivas' goals were lofty but reasonable. They'd tackled their cash flow needs and made tentative plans for how they wanted to use their money in their lifetimes and beyond. They'd also considered how they wanted to help their children, future generations, and others.

"God has been good to us," Peg said. "It's fun to think of how we might be able to take some of our good fortune and spread it around a bit."

Peg picked up her *People* magazine. "Now if you don't mind, I need to catch up on Brad and Angie," she quipped.

Rich leaned his head back against the seat and scanned his eyes across the aisles of fellow passengers. Most of them were graying or balding, he noted. He wondered if they were all as preoccupied with financial planning as he had become. Were they all as organized as they appeared, or were they as confused as Rich felt at times?

Rich thought about the financial planning process. He found truth in the old cliché: The more he understood, the more he realized he didn't understand. Ironically, few on the airplane had the net worth of Peg and Rich, and only a handful had seriously contemplated their financial future to the extent that the Vivas had.

Rich's plans were coming together, regardless of his self-doubt. It was a classic example of the nagging voice from within being one's own worst critic. After all, they had just made a breakthrough by determining what they wanted to accomplish for generations to come. These decisions would make a difference in their lives, in their children's and grandchildren's lives, and in the lives of people they would never even know by name. They were well on their way.

Chapter 5

Risk Tolerance

Rich Viva needed to get back to Houston by Saturday so he could drive to his hometown of Bryan for a reunion celebration at his old high school. The twin cities of Bryan and College Station are located 90 miles northwest of Houston and are best known for Rich's alma mater, Texas A&M University. When Rich was a high school student in the early 1970s, Bryan High School was the heart of the tight-knit community in central Texas, second in prominence only to Texas A&M. Bryan High School still served as a rallying point for students like Rich who had moved away. Former students and teachers held reunions every few years to see their old friends and reconnect with the community.

"I wonder how my old teachers are faring these days," Rich said as he and Peg drove in their SUV through the outskirts of Houston. "From what I heard, I expect at least a few of them to be there."

This was the first Bryan High reunion in six years. Some of Rich's old classmates who still lived in Bryan organized the reunions, not based on anniversaries, but for special events or just when they got around to it. Rich had been particularly looking forward to this event—a tribute to the old teachers.

"It's hard to imagine that any teacher who's old enough to have taught you would still be alive," Peg said playfully.

Rich laughed. "I know it. But all the teachers were women in those days, and women tend to live longer than men."

"That's a good point," Peg said. "And it's another reason our financial plan is so important to me."

"Fair enough," Rich said. "What, you don't want to go back to work after I die? I think you still have plenty of marketable skills."

"Maybe so, but I'd rather focus on getting our investments in good order," Peg responded. "I think the next step is to consider our risk tolerance."

Rich thought about risk tolerance as he drove northwest from Houston through the rolling wooded hills and cattle ranch country. Ernie, Sally Victor, and the financial advisor had all made repeated references to risk tolerance. It refers to how much market volatility and high-risk holdings an investor is comfortable with in his portfolio.

The financial advisor had suggested a moderate approach. That sounded good in theory, Rich thought, but it also contradicted part of his thinking when it came to business. Rich attributed the success of his business largely to the substantial risks he had taken, most of which paid off. Like the time he invested nearly $3 million— equal to the value of his business at the time—into researching and developing an innovative compression technology. The new machine ended up working great, and his business thrived as a result. Would his business have survived under a moderate approach?

This was a new financial era for the Vivas, however—an era in which there would be no regular income from the business. Rich didn't want to be unnecessarily risky with the savings that he and Peg were reliant on for the rest of their lives.

"There are two things that I can think of that could go wrong along those lines," Peg said. "I have a hard time believing we would outlive $16 million. But we could gamble our savings away on risky investments, or we could be so conservative that our money doesn't keep up with inflation or allow us any luxuries, or leave anything for the kids."

"I hear you," Rich said. "This is the notion that's haunted me since I signed the contract to sell the business. It's funny. I never could have imagined $16 million as a young man. But now we're worried that we'll outlive it. I guess when it comes to risk tolerance, it's about striking that balance."

The Vivas soon arrived at Bryan High, an enormous campus that had grown over the years along with the city's population. Rich hardly recognized the massive building and almost felt lost finding the cafeteria where the reunions were held. Rich parked the car. "Here we go," he said. "I better not be the oldest alumnus here. I sure hope a lot of us old students made it to honor these teachers."

When contacted about the reunion, Rich had agreed to cover the cost of catering the event and volunteered to introduce his 10th-grade math teacher, Mrs. Lucille Sharpwell.

Over the years, Rich had become accustomed to donating money, and he stepped up to lead various projects for civic and nonprofit groups. The good will and publicity generated by such activity could be good for business every once in a while. In the end, he felt that it was his privilege to have the means to help out when and where he could with causes that he and Peg believed in and wanted to support.

However, as soon as the business sale hit the papers, it seemed that there were endless requests from those looking for money. It wasn't that the organizations weren't deserving of contributions, but there's a limit to what one can donate. If he and Peg bought a table at every charity gala they were invited to, he wouldn't need to worry about all the extra cash from the sale of the business, because there wouldn't be much left over.

For the first time Rich could understand the need to create a foundation or charitable trust, as so many of the truly wealthy had done. Peg had read that the most productive way to donate is to concentrate gifts to a limited number of worthwhile charities, because your gift can be more impactful for those you select. It was hard for Rich to imagine establishing a foundation or charitable trust, but he thought it could be worth looking into someday.

Picking up the barbecue lunch was a small expense and he was happy to give to a group of people that had been so instrumental in making him the man he had become. For Rich, top of the list of those folks was Mrs. Sharpwell. If a cheap catering bill made the day for his favorite teacher, and for others from his early life, he was in for that 100 percent.

Mrs. Sharpwell, now in her late 70s, was an innovative and engaging teacher who could draw the best from her students while making school fun. In preparation for the reunion, Rich had called her to catch up and get some details about her life over the years. Mrs. Sharpwell seemed to be quite happy. She and her husband, Johnny Sharpwell, had recently celebrated their golden wedding anniversary and were enjoying retirement in a comfortable home at Pebble Creek golf course. Rich was impressed with his former teacher's apparent comfort and peace of mind. He looked forward to seeing her in person for the first time in many years.

As he and Peg entered the cafeteria, Rich scanned the room to assess the turnout. He felt a tugging at his elbow. He turned to see a stooped, gray-headed woman in a formal but well-worn blue polyester dress. Her nametag read, "Martha Hamilton, history teacher."

Sure enough, it was old Miss Hamilton. She was offering coffee in Styrofoam cups. Rich and Peg took the last two cups from the plastic tray.

"Thank you, Richard," Miss Hamilton said. "Now let's catch up before I get lassoed for another chore."

Rich was delighted to see Miss Hamilton. He gave her a big hug and then grabbed three folding metal chairs for them to sit down and chat.

Rich, Peg, and Miss Hamilton visited for the better part of 15 minutes as the room filled up with alumni, teachers, and others from the community. Miss Hamilton talked about how she had retired 15 years earlier and was living out her years in Bryan at a slow pace. They were interrupted when the catering company announced that the barbecue lunch was ready.

There was no shortage on good barbecue restaurants in that part of Texas; Bryan-College Station had some great ones. But since he was covering the bill, Rich chose Red River BBQ out of Houston. The restaurant had catered ACS client and employee events over the years and he knew the owners would make certain it was done right. Red River was one of the few barbecue restaurants that still used only wood to smoke their delicious brisket, and he knew they would be happy to drive to Bryan for one of their favorite customers. He would not be disappointed.

Rich and Peg filled their trays with plates of brisket, rolls, and coleslaw. They each grabbed a cup of iced tea from the counter and took seats at a circular table where Rich recognized a couple of his old classmates. The acquaintances were catching up and discussing current events like the latest local politics in Bryan and the Texas A&M Aggie football team. That's when another teacher approached the table. It was Judy Kenneth, Rich's biology teacher.

Rich greeted his former teacher, who looked surprisingly aged compared to when he had last seen her about 20 years before. "Well," Rich thought, "she is in her late 70s." Like the Vivas, Ms. Kenneth lived in Houston. Rich was surprised to hear that Ms. Kenneth was still working as a secretary and office manager at a small oil exploration company. He remembered that, 20 years earlier, she was doing quite well as an executive assistant at Hatfield Energy Corp. and planning to retire.

"So you're still working these days?" Rich asked her.

"It's a long story," Ms. Kenneth said. "I won't bore you with the details."

Peg changed the subject. "Are you staying for the night, or did you just drive in for the day?" she asked.

Ms. Kenneth was staying with her cousin, who had given her a ride from the Greyhound bus stop to Bryan High, and who planned to pick her up when the party was over.

"Why don't we give you a ride to your cousin's house?" Peg offered. Ms. Kenneth accepted.

It was time for the program to begin. There were nine teachers present who had taught at Bryan High in the early 1970s. Former students introduced each teacher with short tributes, and then the teachers had an opportunity to say a few words.

Rich executed his tribute to Mrs. Sharpwell according to plan. He talked about her pleasant demeanor, as well as the sharp disciplinarian she could become when provoked by relentless sophomores. Rich recalled the time he played a prank on a classmate by tampering with a classmate's desk so it collapsed when the student sat down.

"I fully acknowledge it was out of line," Rich said. "And the punishment was steep."

Mrs. Sharpwell had assigned the victim to Rich's desk while Rich was ordered to stand throughout class for a week.

"I tell you, I sure got the message," Rich said. "I haven't tampered with anyone's chair ever since. I sometimes wonder if that kind of effective discipline would fly today."

At the conclusion of the program, the students surprised their teachers with sweater vests with the Bryan Viking school logo on the back and their names stitched on the front. The ladies were thrilled. It was a joyous affair. Everybody agreed that the event was a success.

The Vivas milled around the cafeteria for another hour or so, visiting mostly with Mrs. Sharpwell and her husband, Johnny. As the afternoon wore into evening, they found Ms. Kenneth and drove her to her cousin's house.

Rich took the chance to ask his old teacher about her life. She told him about her husband's unexpected death from cancer 19 years before. She also talked about her career at Hatfield Energy Corp., a big player in the energy industry that had folded under corrupt management, and her decision to keep working at a smaller, family-owned firm.

The Vivas dropped off Ms. Kenneth at her cousin's house, bid farewell, and motored on to the bed and breakfast at Messina Hof, a local winery and vineyard.

The Vivas had become big wine fans in recent years. They didn't call themselves connoisseurs, but they liked the subtleties, sophistication, and heritage of the beverage. Messina Hof was a favorite destination—a picturesque vineyard, winery, and estate that actually produced pretty decent wine. It was an unexpected central Texas gem. They checked into their room and headed to one of the outdoor garden wine patios. Rich ordered a Cabernet Sauvignon, and Peg decided on a Sauvignon Blanc.

It had been a long day. "It's interesting how those three teachers' lives turned out, isn't it?" Rich said.

Mrs. Sharpwell had it pretty good, while Ms. Kenneth and Miss Hamilton seemed to be scraping by.

"I hope we're more like the Sharpwells in 20 years," he said.

Peg spoke up. "I can tell you're obsessing over this 'risk tolerance' idea based on the questions you asked those ladies. I bet they didn't realize they were going to be interviewed about their financial planning strategies."

The teacher's experiences represented interesting differences, Peg said, specifically related to risk tolerance.

"What do you mean by that?" Rich asked.

Peg explained her interpretation of the three examples.

Johnny and Lucille Sharpwell held normal middle-class jobs, she as a teacher for her entire career and he as a civil engineer in the Bryan city government's planning department. When they were in their 30s, they developed an investment plan to make the most of the little amount of money they were able to invest on a monthly basis.

They worked with a financial advisor who encouraged them to take a moderate approach with a comfortable amount of risk. They built a diversified investment portfolio comprised mostly of stocks, and also including bonds and a rainy-day cash fund. They eventually bought their own house and also acquired two others in town, rental properties, both of which had been in the family

The Sharpwells stuck to their investment plan, taking only moderate levels of risk to grow their portfolio and resisting the temptation to go exclusively with hot stocks during boom cycles.

Their rainy-day fund was a major help when Johnny was out of work for a year in the 1980s, during the savings and loan crisis, when the city of Bryan slashed its operating budget and temporarily furloughed Johnny and several other employees. At the time, the Sharpwells were tempted to cash out their investments and put their money in a savings account, but they held out and maintained their investments.

It had paid off. Now they lived on a golf course and took annual vacations to interesting places. That summer, they'd gone on an Alaskan cruise, and the summer before they'd toured Germany.

The Sharpwells had nurtured their nest egg through a moderate investment approach and it had worked. They were living their retirement in confidence and comfort based on their retirement plans and income from their portfolio. Their money was going to outlive them.

"Based on what I've heard, I'd say the Sharpwells are doing it by the book," Rich said. "And they're not super wealthy. They're just smart about it."

"I would agree," Peg said. "Now Miss Hamilton, her story was an interesting contrast."

Martha Hamilton also taught school for her entire career, earning enough to support herself modestly throughout her working life. She never married, and seldom took vacations or made luxurious purchases.

Miss Hamilton had learned about stock market investing at a teacher convention in Austin back in the 1960s. But the stock market scared her. A child of the Depression, her father had hammered home the idea of saving money and, as he put it, "avoiding the foolish and risky stock market that had burned an entire American generation." (See Exhibit 5.1.)

Miss Hamilton saved part of her money in a savings account and also invested in several certificates of deposit. She'd been tempted to venture into more aggressive investing, especially when the market was climbing. However, she'd talked herself out of taking any risk, assuring herself that her conservative approach was the safest.

Miss Hamilton slept easily at night, never feeling the impact of market pullbacks like some of her friends with money in the stock market. But things changed after she retired 15 years earlier. She had her cash savings, but the cost of everything, from food to property taxes on her small home, were going up.

Her leash got shorter by the year as her cash savings dropped and she relied increasingly on Social Security. Now she was looking at the possibility of moving into a retirement community, but the rent wasn't cheap and she wasn't sure she could afford it.

Miss Hamilton acknowledged that she had no one to blame but herself. Still, she couldn't help but feel a bit resentful of her mother and father, who constantly stressed the perils of investing in the market.

"For all intents and purposes, she has outlived her money," Peg said. "It's heartbreaking because it's sad to see an elderly woman in

The worst 10-year return period since the 1930s

10-year moving annualized nominal returns, 1839 to 2011*

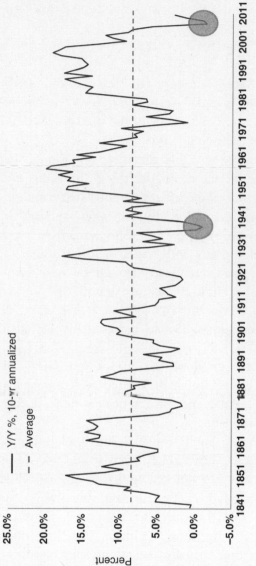

Annualized rolling 10-year nominal returns

Past performance is no guarantee of future results.
*Note: Returns based on calendar years; calendar year 2011 data updated through December 31, 2011.
Source: Stifel Nicholas. Used with permission. For 1826 through 1925: Combined individual stock prices for NYSE stocks. Goetzmann, William N., Ibbotson, Roger G. and Peng, Liang, A New Historical Database for the NYSE 1815 To 1925: Performance and Predictability (July 14, 2000). Yale ICF Working Paper No. 00-13; Yale SOM Working Paper No. ICF -00-13. Available at SSRN: http://ssrn.com/abstract=236982. For 1926 to 1958, Ibbotson Large Capitalization US stock market total return and in subsequently, the S&P 500 total return.

Exhibit 5.1 Rarely does the market experience a decade of negative returns. We all want to learn from our mistakes, but we must be careful in the lessons we take from our experiences. If we're not careful, we may learn the wrong lesson, as Miss Hamilton's father did back in the Great Depression.

financial distress. And she could have avoided it. She made enough money to plan for the future, but she was too spooked by investing to do it."

Rich nodded. "It's interesting that she now realizes where she went wrong," he said.

Unfortunately, Miss Hamilton had learned the hard way that outliving your money is equally as dangerous—if not more so—than living with volatility and fluctuations in the markets. (See Exhibit 5.2.)

"What about Ms. Kenneth?" Rich asked.

"I think her story is probably the most interesting," Peg said. "It seems like she had good intentions, but things just didn't work out for her. It's another sad story, but different from Miss Hamilton's."

Judy Kenneth left Bryan for Houston after working as a teacher for four years at Bryan High School. She wanted to try something different—life in the big city and perhaps another career.

Her adventure started out great. Hatfield Energy Corp. hired her as a secretary, and she found a nice apartment. She loved the social life and excitement of the big city. Within a few years, she married Bob Cernosek, a geologist who was working his way up the ladder at Hatfield.

Judy and Bob lived the good life in Houston. They had a healthy combined income. They never had children, and followed their interests in collecting art, sailing, and traveling to exotic places in the world, such as Africa and Thailand.

When Hatfield went public in 1975, Judy and Bob invested their family savings in Hatfield shares. They knew it was risky to put all their eggs in one basket, and they ignored advice to diversify. Judy and Bob understood the idea of diversification, but they were confident in Hatfield. They also knew that they didn't want to outlive their money in later years, so at the time it made sense to them to risk their savings by investing virtually everything they had in Hatfield.

It didn't feel like a risky decision at the time. Hatfield was growing exponentially, and enthusiasm at the Houston headquarters was infectious. Their portfolio value was growing quickly, and they were making money.

Then things fell apart. Bob was diagnosed with cancer in 1991 and died within six months. Judy was devastated, but she remained

Equities have protected purchasing power over time

Growth of $10,000 from 1925 to December 31, 2011

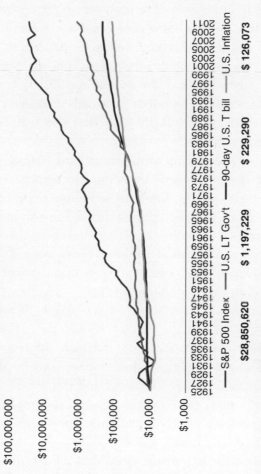

S&P 500 Index	$28,850,620
U.S. LT Gov't	$1,197,229
90-day U.S. T bill	$229,290
U.S. Inflation	$126,073

Note: $10,000 may not be representative of a typical investment in 1925.

Source: Ned Davis Research; used with permission. **The chart is shown for illustrative purposes only, and is not meant to show the returns of any particular UBS Global Asset Management investment.** Stocks represented by Standard & Poor's (S&P) 500 Index, long-term government bonds by 20-year US Treasury bonds, 90-day US Treasury bills and inflation by the Consumer Price Index (CPI through December 31, 2011). The S&P 500 Index is an unmanaged, weighted index comprising 500 widely held common stocks varying in composition. Returns consist of income, capital appreciation (or depreciation) and currency gains (or losses). Certain markets have experienced significant year-to-year fluctuations and negative returns from time to time. Stocks are more volatile and subject to greater risks than other asset classes. Indexes are not available for direct investment. **Past performance is not a guarantee of future results.**

Exhibit 5.2 Over extended periods of time, equities have greatly outperformed long-term U.S. treasuries, short-term U.S. treasury bills, and inflation.

in good financial shape because Hatfield had performed pretty well. Then Hatfield began to unravel. Three years later, in 1994, Hatfield collapsed under mismanagement and an accounting scandal. The once-mighty company shut its doors within a year, and its stock price fell to pennies.

Ms. Kenneth's life savings were reduced to almost nothing. She wasn't completely destitute; Bob's life insurance policy provided some income. But she and Bob had also developed a comfortable lifestyle that she had a difficult time affording. To her credit, Ms. Kenneth had picked up the pieces and found another secretarial job. She had out-lived her savings and was paying her way at age 77.

"It's interesting that Ms. Kenneth and Miss Hamilton now find themselves at a similar place," Rich said, "because their investment strategies were quite different."

Both had failed when it came to investing: Miss Hamilton by being too conservative and Ms. Kenneth by being too aggressive. Although the outcome was the same, Ms. Kenneth somehow felt more justified in her decision-making. Had her plan worked, life would have been so different for her.

"Miss Hamilton also felt as if she was being a good steward of what little she did have," Peg noted. "It's just that she had not taken the effects of inflation into consideration."

"So what's the moral of the story?" Rich asked. "It seems pretty clear to me."

He said the Sharpwells had chosen the right strategy by taking moderate investment risks to grow their money and by diversifying their investments among a range of stocks and bonds.

"The Sharpwells didn't put all their chips on red or black like Ms. Kenneth did," Peg responded. "Nor did they bury it under the proverbial mattress like Miss Hamilton did."

The Sharpwells made logical decisions that ended up making the difference between the comfortable lifestyle they were now living and the uncertainty imposed upon the two other teachers.

It was clear to Rich which outcome he and Peg should strive for.

"So you're pointing to these examples to say that we should take on a reasonable risk tolerance level for our portfolio?" Rich asked.

Peg nodded. "Bingo. And by the way, I have a surprise for you, something to celebrate the business sale. There's a reason I wanted to stay at this winery—a little preview of sorts," she said, pulling a sheet of paper from her purse.

It was a travel reservation for a trip to Sonoma County in three weeks.

"I know you've always wanted to see California wine country," Peg said. "Let's enjoy our Texas wine and then go see how they make wine in California."

Rich was taken aback. "Wow, what a trip," he said. "You're right that it's been a dream of mine. What a trip!"

"Yes," Peg responded. "I absolutely love this sense of freedom."

Rich's stomach churned. He'd only stepped away from the office a few weeks before. He'd already been on a two-week trip to Wyoming, and now had plans for a California vacation. Were they spending their money too fast? Burning through their savings? Outspending their investment income?

Rich took a sip of wine, put on a smile, and nodded.

"Yes. This freedom, it's quite a feeling."

Chapter 6

Asset Allocation
and Meritage

Peg had long dreamed of taking a trip with Rich to California wine country to tour various wineries and soak in the culture. She imagined a land of laid-back and sophisticated people with plenty of time on their hands to discuss and enjoy the finer parts of life. What better time to visit than when they finally had some leisure time?

Peg and Rich had become wine fans over the previous 15 years as the beverage grew in popularity and became a featured part of the various dinners and parties they attended. They loved the nuances of different wines, and the fact that you could drink a glass or two without ruining your appetite.

Every time they began to think about a trip to Sonoma, however, their busy lives would interfere and the notion would be sidelined. There was always something related to Rich's work, the kids, their parents, or their various commitments in Houston.

Rich's business sale provided a unique opportunity, Peg thought, and she jumped at the chance. She did some research and made a week's reservation at a chateau at the Shady Oaks vineyard and winery in the heart of wine country. She chose Shady Oaks because it produced the couple's favorite Meritage, Shady's Secret. She didn't tell Rich in advance, wanting to surprise him with the tickets.

Peg sensed Rich's unease with their newfound freedom and footloose travel plans. She realized it would be an adjustment for him. The husbands of several of her friends had retired in recent years, and they always seemed to encounter a retirement crisis of sorts, at least in the beginning. With time, though, most of them adjusted to a new lifestyle that reflected their personalities.

Some of the men fell in love with free time and spent their time as quietly as possible. Others got the travel bug and spent their days either traveling or planning their next trip. Still others found ways to parlay their interests into second jobs, like the fellow who served as commissioner of the recreational basketball league. Many of the retirees didn't really retire; they stayed in the field with consulting companies related to their old jobs.

Peg recalled a *Wall Street Journal* article from many years back about the average life expectancy of retired chief executive officers of publicly traded companies. The story told of people who had retired from all-encompassing and stressful jobs, like Rich's job at ACS. Apparently, some of the retirees found little reason to live, unless they found another place to focus their efforts and time. Peg didn't want Rich to die young, nor did she want him hanging around the house 24/7.

Peg knew Rich would have to adjust, and she was prepared to help him. She was curious to see what he decided to do with his time. She had only a few rules for Rich in the new phase of his life:

1) She wanted him to have a purpose to get up each day looking forward to what life would bring. She knew he would be unfulfilled without a sense of meaning or purpose.
2) She didn't want him getting carried away with talk radio.
3) She didn't want him to fret about money all the time.

In the short time since the business sale, travel had taken up most of Rich's time. He was enjoying it because it was a great opportunity to spend time with Peg and relax away from Houston. Rich knew that he would get restless sitting around the house, but he hadn't really had to face that yet.

During their flight to San Francisco, Rich was thumbing through the shopping magazine that he found in the back seat pocket. One of the featured items was an acoustic guitar for $200. Rich felt a surprising urge to order one. He hadn't played a musical instrument since those few years he played trumpet in the high school band, nor had he felt compelled to try to play music since then.

"I think I might take up the guitar," Rich said, turning to Peg.

"That'll be the day," Peg said. Then she caught her skepticism and reeled it back in. "But that could definitely be a good way to pass time. Does Ernie play any instruments? Maybe you two could form a band? You could call it Fogey Force."

"I don't get it," Rich said, deadpan. "It would be hard to form a band without any ability to play. I'm just thinking it would be fun to play around with a guitar. I haven't had the time or inclination since high school."

"I think you should go for it," Peg said. "Maybe we'll see one in California that you'd like to buy."

Upon arrival, they rented a convertible and drove up the picturesque coastline into wine country. The very atmosphere of the place conveyed a sense of relaxation. Rich wondered why they hadn't taken the time to do this before.

Their room at the Shady Oaks chateau was quiet and comfortable, not overly stuffy, and had a window looking out over acres of green vineyards. They had spent their first day touring two nearby wineries. For day two, they were scheduled for an "insider's tour" of Shady Oaks. The insider's tour was limited to visitors who lodged on site. It featured an extensive presentation of the winemaking process, including the vineyard and the winery.

The tour made for a fascinating day. Rich likened it to a condensed college class, crammed full of details about history, agriculture, and chemistry. To the Vivas' delight, the tour included a presentation by Will Frederick, the master winemaker behind Shady Oaks' annual batch of Shady's Secret. Will was a Sonoma County native who'd been working at vineyards since he was in his teens. At 55, he had the dark, weather-beaten countenance of a man who'd worked out-doors all of his life.

Meritage, the American version of French Bordeaux, is a blended wine made by mixing other labels. Will explained how the winery mixed its Cabernet Sauvignon, Cabernet Franc, and Merlot each year to come up with the perfect blend. Will said the winery didn't aim for radical change each year. Rather, it tried to preserve the hallmarks of the Meritage's distinctive taste while introducing new elements for diversity and improvement.

"How do you introduce new elements?" Rich asked. "Is it a matter of altering the percentage of each type of wine, or do you mean adding other ingredients?"

Will replied that any alterations made each year would be minor. His goal was to make each batch of Shady's Secret interesting in its own right each year, but 10 years down the road, he would want the product to be recognizable as the same label. Alterations could include changing the blend percentages, adding small amounts of other variet-ies, or making other changes related to fermentation.

"We feel like we know what works for Shady's Secret," Will said. "Nevertheless, the public's taste changes over time, and so we bring in new people every year to give their two cents.

"For example, I invite new employees to give their input when we're preparing the annual blend. A lot of those folks come to work for us because they love Shady's Secret, so they always have strong opinions. I also tour the country from time to time to promote our winery, so I take the chance to invite local sommeliers to give their input on recent vintages and their opinions on how we might improve it," he said.

"And each year, I'll try putting a little bit of one of the previous year's batches into the new blend, just to see if it works. Maybe it's my imagination, but I often find that imparts a certain authenticity and timelessness to the new blend."

"Do you know of any wineries that overhaul their Meritage from year to year?" Rich asked.

"Not really," Will responded. "I've seen a few companies do it, but that's only because their Meritage sold poorly and they needed to go another direction, or a new owner took over and wanted to make his own mark."

As the tour moved on, Rich thought about the fact that Shady's Secret changed slightly from year to year. He had never noticed the difference in taste, which he mentioned to Peg.

"Me neither, to be honest with you," Peg said. "But for the past few years that we've been buying Shady's Secret, I can tell you that I'm always curious and excited to try it again. Maybe that's because it's always a little different. It keeps me on my toes, but it's so subtle that I hadn't thought about it before."

Rich chuckled at his wife's analysis, although he readily agreed with her. "Maybe you should apply for a job here. You seem to really be getting into the spirit."

The insider's tour concluded with a four-course dinner on a private patio of the chateau, featuring Shady Oaks' finest wines paired with each course. The sun was sinking over the mountain in the distance, and the waning light cast a golden shadow over the green rows of grape vines. Rich felt content.

"I think this day alone was worth whatever we paid for this vacation," he said as he sipped Shady's Secret. "What did this cost, by the way?"

"Don't worry about it," Peg said. "You'll have to trust me that it's not going to break us. Have you forgotten that you just made $12 million on the business sale?"

Rich shook his head. "No. But I can't imagine living like a multi-millionaire," he said. "With any luck, we'll have plenty of time to spend that money, and hopefully not outlive it."

Since their trip to the Bryan High School reunion, Rich had been thinking about the importance of risk in investing and how it had made a difference in the lives of his three favorite former teachers. Each had experienced drastically different outcomes as result of their risk tolerance. Peg noticed that the example of the teachers had not comforted Rich as she had hoped it would. He may have gained some confidence in the Sharpwells' example of proper financial management, but the experiences of his other teachers saddened him and amplified his apprehension about making the right choices for their lives and their descendants.

Peg took a final bite of crème brûlée and thought about the situation. She had hoped the trip would help distract Rich from his retirement money concerns, but he was developing this annoying habit of somehow relating everything to stress over finances. She could see the gears spinning in Rich's head. "Let's see if I can head him off at the pass," Peg thought to herself.

"Were you thinking about our finances all day?" she asked.

"Not all day, but from time to time," Rich said. He'd been too engaged in the particulars of Shady Oaks' winemaking process to be overly distracted by financial concerns.

"That's probably a good thing," Peg continued. "Because I was distracted by the parallels between the Meritage blend and asset allocation."

Rich lifted his glass of Shady's Secret and peered through it.

"I don't see it," he said. "Has all the tasting gotten to you?"

"No. Hear me out."

Asset allocation is the financial term for an investor's allotment of money within his portfolio. There are four different asset classes in a portfolio: equities, bonds, cash, and alternative investments. Most investors strive to build a portfolio with a diversity of assets that work together toward the goals of producing returns and limiting risk.

Equity is another word for stock. Equities represent ownership in a company. Bonds are synonymous with fixed income, or debt. A bond is similar to a loan to a company. When you buy a bond issued by a company, you're loaning that company a certain amount of cash. Assuming the company lives up to its end of the bargain and doesn't default on the loan, the company ultimately repays the cash along with interest. Cash is obviously the green stuff, but it is also money market holdings and extremely liquid short-term paper, which are investments in short-term debt obligations with very short maturities. Alternative investments are things out of the ordinary, such as hedge funds, private equity, and commodities.

"Remember how Will Frederick explained how he blends different kinds of wines to make the Meritage you're drinking right now?" Peg said. She paused to see if Rich was following her. "That's how an investor blends different kinds of investments to build a good portfolio." (See Exhibit 6.1.)

Asset allocation is essential

UBS asset allocation study

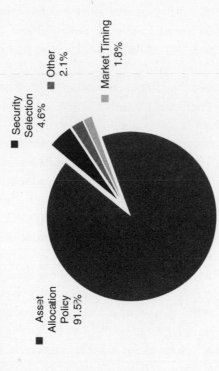

Asset Allocation Policy 91.5%

Security Selection 4.6%

Other 2.1%

Market Timing 1.8%

Bottom Line: According to this study, asset allocation—America's most admired, but least practiced investment discipline—accounts for 91.5% of the variation in portfolio returns.[1]

Conclusion: Strategic asset allocation can help manage portfolio risk while stabilizing returns.[2]

1 Gary P. Brinson, L. Randolph Hood and Gilbert L. Beebower, "Determinants of Portfolio Performance," *The Financial Analysts Journal*, July/August 1986; and Gary P. Brinson, Brian D. Singer and Gilbert L. Beebower, "Determinants of Portfolio Performance II: An Update,"*The Financial Analysts Journal*, May/June 1991.
2 Asset allocation, however, does not assure a profit or prevent loss from occurring in an investment portfolio.

Exhibit 6.1   Sometimes investors focus on issues that don't have a significant impact on their portfolio. A focus on asset allocation will have more of an impact on a portfolio than most other issues.

Rich smiled. He had learned that Peg knew her stuff when it came to finances, but she didn't rub it in his face unless she felt it was worthwhile. So he listened.

"When we build our portfolio, we're going to need to decide on an asset allocation that makes sense for our goals," Peg said.

Peg's comparison related to the equity class, but it could also relate to the overall asset allocation among various investment classes, as well. To reach his goals, an investor needs to choose the right mix of large-, mid- and small-cap stocks, growth and value stocks, as well as domestic and international stocks.

"That's similar to how Shady Oaks selects the right allocation of Cabernet Sauvignon, Cab Franc, and Merlot when they blend them together to make Shady's Secret Meritage," Peg noted.

"Fortunately, we can get help with this, and it's not all up to us to develop the blend," Peg said, and added quickly, "However, I can already anticipate some of the investments we should consider for inclusion."

"For us, that's probably going to mean a relatively conservative mix that protects our wealth but is also active enough to grow our money and meet our lifelong needs," Peg said.

"That sounds great," Rich said. "You make it seem so simple and logical. I need to write that down and tape it to my forehead."

"Let's not get carried away," Peg said. "After all, people with the best of intentions make financial mistakes all of the time.

"But asset allocation can help make up for mistakes," Peg said. "And perhaps this could be compared to Meritage as well."

She continued: "For example, if Shady Oaks' Cabernet Sauvignon turns out bad one year, they can't sell any of it or use it in their Meritage. But the winery could still salvage its Meritage by replacing the Cabernet Sauvignon component with a similar wine from another reliable source. This is similar to a portfolio that has only one asset class. If an investor's small-cap value stocks do poorly one year and all his holdings are in that one area, then it would disrupt his entire portfolio. But if small-cap value stocks are only one part of the total, say five percent, then a rough year for those stocks won't seriously hurt the portfolio. The important part is the diversification of assets.

Diversification

America's most admired, least practiced investment discipline

The Callan Periodic Table of Annual Investment Returns for Selected Asset Classes (1990 to December 31, 2011)
Ranked from Best to Worst Performance

1990 1991 1992 1993 1994 1995 1996 1997 1998 1999 2000 2001 2002 2003 2004 2005 2006 2007 2008 2009 2010 2011

■ **Small Cap Value**, represented by the Russell 2000 Value Index, contains those Russell 2000 securities with a less-than-average growth orientation. Securities in this index generally have lower price-to-book and price-to-earnings ratios than those in the Russell 2000 Growth Index.

■ **Small Cap Growth**, represented by the Russell 2000 Growth Index, contains those Russell 2000 securities with a greater-than-average growth orientation. Securities in this index generally have higher price-to-book and price-to-earnings ratios than those in the Russell 2000 Value Index.

■ **International Stocks**, represented by the MSCI EAFE Index, is a Morgan Stanley Capital International index that is designed to measure the performance of the developed stock markets of Europe, Australasia, and the Far East.

■ **Large Cap Stocks**, represented by the Russell 1000 Index, which measures the performance of the 1,000 largest companies in the Russell 3000 Index.

■ **Large Cap Growth** and ■ **Large Cap Value**, represented by the Russell 1000 Growth and the Russell 1000 Value indexes. The Russell 1000 Growth Index measures the performance of those Russell 1000 companies with higher price-to-book ratios and higher forecasted growth values. The Russell 1000 Value Index measures the performance of those Russell 1000 companies with lower price-to-book ratios and lower forecasted growth values.

■ **US Bonds**, represented by the Barclays Capital U.S. Aggregate Bond Index, includes US government, corporate, and mortgage-backed securities with maturities up to 30 years.

■ **Small Cap Stocks**, represented by the Russell 2000 Index. The Russell 2000 is a market-value-weighted index of the 2,000 smallest stocks in the broad-market Russell 3000 Index. These securities are traded on the NYSE, AMEX and NASDAQ.

■ **Equity Market Neutral**, represented by the HFRI Equity Market Neutral Index, an equally weighted index designed to measure the performance of equity market neutral hedge funds in the internal HFR Database.

Source: UBS Global Asset Management.

Data as of 12/31/11. For illustrative purposes only. Security incices are unmanaged. They assume reinvestment of distributions and interest payments and do not take into account fees, taxes and other charges. Such fees and charges would reduce performance. It is not possible to invest directly in an index. Past performance does not guarantee future results.

Exhibit 6.2 The performance of asset classes changes regularly. As a result, it behooves investors to diversify among various asset classes. This lessens the blow of a major pullback in one specific class and also provides guidance on the areas an investor may want to marginally overweight or underweight.

In the case of a Meritage or an investment portfolio, diversification protects the whole from problematic parts." (See Exhibit 6.2.)

"I see what you're getting at," Rich said. "I think diversification makes a lot of sense."

"And it varies from person to person," Peg added. "Just like goals and objectives, and risk tolerance. For someone like our son, Patrick, the asset allocation will be more aggressive, because he's got time in his life to take more risks."

Rich nodded and chuckled.

"You should definitely make this case to him. He needs a lesson in finances, and a lesson based in alcohol might actually get through to him."

"You could also take it a step further," Peg said. She was rolling now and she took a dignified sip of wine to drive home the point.

"Today, Will talked about the maceration process and how much time the grape seeds, stems, and skin are kept with the fermenting grape juice. Changing the skin contact time changes the wine's flavor. Leaving it longer gives it a darker flavor. Removing it quickly gives it a lighter flavor. That's like diversifying your portfolio between value stocks and growth stocks."

Value stocks tend to be old, healthy companies that generally produce dividends, but are no longer growing. Growth stocks tend to be younger companies that aren't paying dividends, but whose stock's value is going up as the company invests its capital back into growth. The differentiation sometimes blurs, as there are times when growth stocks have value characteristics and when value stocks have growth characteristics.

In a flat equity market, dividend yields may produce the only returns, whereas in a rising market, more growth-oriented holdings may appreciate faster than high-dividend-yielding stocks.

A properly allocated portfolio will have both value and growth stocks, but the amount of each will change depending on the investor's goals and the economic cycle. Likewise, a winemaker will shorten or lengthen the maceration process to produce different flavors of wine. In the case of a Meritage, the different wines are blended together with the ultimate goal of creating the distinctive taste.

"Like the Shady's Secret that we love," Peg said.

Rich was thinking about Peg's analogy.

"There's one point that I think really applies to both Meritage and asset allocation," he said. "That's the idea of maintaining some consistency while also looking for slight variations that can make your wine, or your portfolio, better. Will talked about how they don't change the Shady's Secret blend much from year to year, and most smart investors don't tinker too much with their portfolio either," Rich said. "You don't need to reinvent the wheel all the time; at least, that's what Ernie Troutman told me. He said you're normally better off sticking with a stable and diversified portfolio, and then you can make slight modifications from time to time optimize your returns."

Peg agreed. She had read about famous investors who made bold, wholesale decisions moving from one asset class to another, but she felt that gradual moves and a more moderate approach would allow them to sleep better at night.

Peg brought up an example about her sister, Nancy, who tended to make rash decisions.

"Remember when Nancy decided to eliminate international stocks from her portfolio and then the American economy tanked?" Peg queried. "I think we're saying that dumping all of your international stocks would be like leaving the Cab Franc out of the Meritage, which would kill your final product."

It made sense to Rich. The sum of the whole is better than its parts, whether it's Meritage or a portfolio.

"You want to build each part to be great on its own, but they're still stronger as a package," he said. "So then you mix your parts together, either in a portfolio or a bottle of wine. And you can make little modifications to capitalize on market trends, just like little variations on the annual batch of Shady's Secret gives it a little twist each year. But you don't want to make huge changes, because then you're risking making big mistakes."

Peg nodded in agreement. The waiter had taken their plates and they were sipping digestive hot tea.

"This is the best," Peg said, leaning back in her chair. "And have you noticed how when we talk through these financial issues, it normally seems to level your head?"

"It's true," Rich said. "None of this is rocket science, and I don't like to be pessimistic. I feel like I ran Apex Compression Services with a lot of optimism—maybe to a fault, at times.

"We can't afford to put all of our eggs in one basket now that we don't have the time to recover if the basket breaks."

"That's exactly why asset allocation is key to investing. It's the process of placing eggs in several baskets, and choosing the best basket for each different egg," Peg replied.

Rich nodded. "I guess the stakes feel higher now because we're living off a set amount of money," he said. "There's no more income."

"I understand that concern," Peg said. "But if it's any consolation to you, I made the reservations for this trip during your final week of work, so you were still earning income at that time. What's more, when we get our portfolio organized, it will be producing dividends that could pay for this trip in short order."

"I like the sound of that," Rich said. He stood up, stretched, and yawned. "Now we'd better get to sleep. We've got another busy day of wine country touring tomorrow."

Chapter 7

Mechanics of Investing and Winemaking

The Vivas departed Shady Oaks vineyard with a twinge of sadness and nostalgia. Their two-night visit had been a satisfying combination of comfortable and interesting.

"That's going to be hard to beat," Rich said as he drove their rented convertible down Shady Oaks' long gravel driveway and to the highway.

"You never know," Peg said. "There's still a lot to see. I'm hoping we can find another winery tour where we can watch the whole process again. I thought that was fascinating."

"Me, too—and who knew it would turn into a lesson in investing?" Rich responded.

Peg looked across the grassy rolling countryside and tied a veil over her hair to keep it from whipping around in the windy convertible.

"You never know where you're going to find that kind of insight," she said with a wry smile. "You'd be surprised how often it's sitting in the seat right beside you."

"Don't I know it," Rich said as he gunned the convertible down the road.

They were headed about 15 miles north to the next stop on their tour, a fledgling winery called Frais Valley. The wine seller at their local wine shop had recommended Frais Valley to the Vivas a couple of years earlier. They had tried a few of the label's varietals and enjoyed all of them.

Rich pulled the car into the dirt parking lot at Frais Valley's tasting room. A chalkboard on the front wall shared some welcome news: "Winery Tour at 2 pm."

"Excellent! It looks like you're going to get your wish," Rich said. "It will be interesting to compare the operations here to the way Shady Oaks does things."

The Vivas signed up for the tour. They had a couple of hours to wait, so they ordered sandwiches at Frais Valley's tasting room and sampled the local product. They felt like kids in a candy store, gushing with praise for each different wine.

"It always seems to taste better at the source," Rich exclaimed after a sip of Pinot noir.

"That's why we invite people out here." The voice came from an elderly man entering the front door. It was the proprietor, Larry Montclair. He was gearing up for the tour.

It turned out the Vivas had shown up on the right day for a tour, just by coincidence. Larry offered tours only on select occasions when he had the time and energy, and this was one of those days.

Larry joined their table to chat for a few minutes. At age 70, he was in good shape. He wore a full-brimmed straw hat over his bald crown, and he had a close-cropped white beard. His Buddy Holly–style glasses gave him a timeless and trendy image. "Pure California," Rich thought.

A few more tour participants arrived and pulled up chairs to join the conversation.

"Well, it looks like it's time to get started," Larry said. "I like to start the tour with the story of our winery's origins."

Larry, it turned out, had gotten into the winemaking business after a career in transportation logistics in San Francisco. He had acquired the vineyard 20 years earlier, after making a sizeable sum of money in the food delivery business. Larry had spent his adult life in the management office of a refrigerated trucking company that delivered foods to restaurants and grocery stores in the Bay Area. He worked his way up to president of the company, but had always dreamed of owning his own vineyard. He started scouting properties in the early 1990s, and when the Frais Valley property hit the market, he jumped at the chance.

The previous owner had run out of money and energy for the business, Larry said. So Larry changed the name to Frais Valley (*frais* is French for fresh) in homage to the food delivery company he worked for, Fresh Delivery. His wife agreed to the adventure, but only on the condition that they didn't blow their life savings.

"We came close, especially in the early years," Larry said. "It was pretty lean until about 2003, when our name started to get out there and get more recognition. It still amazes me when people like these folks from Houston can buy our wine in Texas and across the country."

Virtually any wine lover with a desire to learn more about wine and winemaking would have enjoyed spending time with Larry Montclair. Rich was impressed with Larry's story, especially the risk he took by leaving his steady job at age 50 to embark on a new adventure. He wanted to learn how Larry had handled his transition from the business world to running a vineyard. If Larry could make a successful transition from one field to another, Rich thought, then he, too, could make a smooth transition into his next phase of life—whatever that was going to be.

The tour continued outside. Larry led the small party to the vineyard to get a close-up look at the grapevines. As they walked across the property, Rich asked Larry how he had the confidence to risk most of his savings on a vineyard.

"It was scary," Larry said. "But I figured I've only got this one life to live. And it helped that my brother is a financial advisor and he kept my investment portfolio on track. My investments aren't huge, but I've always viewed them as a safety net in case the winery goes under. That hasn't happened, thankfully, but I still keep a close eye on my portfolio."

"I don't think you've got to worry about going broke," Rich said. "Frais Valley has a lot of fans."

"I appreciate that. But the world is a fickle place," Larry responded. "What if the grape phylloxera aphid were to come in and wipe out the vineyard? It happened to France in the 1800s. In a matter of a few short years, their industry was wiped out, and it took them a long time to recover.

"I recently visited some friends in Colorado," Larry continued. "And it was amazing to see how the pine beetle infestation is killing swaths of trees across the mountains there."

"We saw that during a trip last year," Rich said. "Pretty sad."

"Sad, but also a natural occurrence," Larry said. "The same thing could happen here with the aphid. Imagine something equally as toxic as the pine beetle munching up all of the grape vines, and you start to get the picture. It would wipe us out."

"That is a scary thought," Rich said.

"And we're not only subject to natural disasters," Larry continued. "The taste of the general public changes all the time. What if palates change significantly and all the wine lovers start drinking craft beer instead?

That drew a chuckle from Rich. "I don't see people giving up on wine. It's been around since before Jesus."

"I hope you're right," Larry said. "I know it sounds far-fetched. But much of what has occurred in the business world recently would have seemed far-fetched, as well. My point is that my investment portfolio is very important to me as a backstop. I want to be ready for whatever might be coming our way."

Rich was impressed with Larry's thoughtful approach. For a seemingly laid-back California winemaker, he had obviously spent a lot of time considering his contingencies. Rich could relate to this. He decided to raise the topic of his business sale. He told Larry about the recent transaction and his concern about developing a new financial plan that he hoped would take he and Peg through the rest of their lives.

"I don't know what kind of beetle or aphid could take us down, but I want to avoid it, whatever it is," Rich said.

Larry listened and nodded his head.

"It is a lot to think about. In fact, during many hours of solo work here on the property, I've developed quite a few thoughts about investing and winemaking. There are a lot of analogies, if you look at it through the right lens," Larry said.

"I seem to have those lenses tightly secured to my eyes," Rich said. "My preoccupation with financial planning seems to find its way into my thoughts and conversations all the time."

"I don't mind," Larry said with a laugh, as the group made its way to the vineyard. "Now let's get down to the nitty-gritty of making the world's finest wine."

Larry's tour included discussion of the history and geography of his vineyard, as well as an explanation of grape farming and the wine-making process. It was another fascinating glimpse at the world the Vivas had wondered about so many times before.

Knowing of Rich's interest, Larry took it upon himself to draw some analogies between winemaking and investing. He pointed out that the geography and climate of a vineyard are like the global and domestic economies that shape investment decisions. In each case, the winemaker and an investor are accessing historical and current data and trends, as well as future outlooks, in pursuit of the best possible outcome.

A winemaker must study the climate of his land, historical weather data, and prevailing weather patterns to determine where he should plant his grapevines and how to position them. Similarly, an investor should start by looking at macro-level indicators—the 30,000-foot view—when making investment decisions.

To figure out if the climate is good for investing, investors should study economic indicators such as gross domestic product, inflation forecast, and the market outlook. They should also look at the Standard & Poor's 500 (S&P 500) as well as other indices to see where the market is trading, and other indicators, such as a stock's P/E ratio, to determine if the market is expensive or inexpensive.

The S&P 500 is a stock index comprised of 10 sectors with a total of 500 companies that are selected to represent the market at large. The S&P 500 was published in 1957 at less than 50 points. Many professional investors believe this index most accurately describes the value of the market in general. The S&P 500 uses a market cap weighting system, meaning that the larger a company is, the greater weighting it has in the index.

Perhaps the most famous of the stock indices is the Dow Jones Industrial Average (DJIA). Initially created in the late 1800s, the DJIA has been comprised of 30 large-company, blue-chip stocks since 1928. Only General Electric has remained in the DJIA since its inception. The Dow uses a price weighting method. As a result, the higher the stock price, the greater its weighting on the index.

Surprisingly, the S&P 500 and DJIA have a correlation of 95 to 96 percent on a quarterly and annual basis, even though one is comprised of 500 companies and is based upon market cap, while the other is only comprised of 30 companies and uses price to determine the weighting of the Dow.

A third stock index is the Nasdaq Composite, which was created in 1971. The Nasdaq Composite is an index made up of nearly 2,800 companies. There's also the Nasdaq 100, known as QQQ, which is comprised of 100 companies. The vast majority of stocks on the Nasdaq indices are technology companies.

For international investing, the Morgan Stanley Capital International Europe, Australasia, and Far East (MSCI EAFE) Index is the quintessential index for international comparison.

For smaller companies, the index that is often used to compare and contract stocks is the Russell 2000. Russell has a number of indices, and the 2000 is often used as a proxy for smaller companies.

Bonds also have various indices. Some of the most prominent are the Barclays Aggregate Bond Index, the Barclays Treasury bond Index, the municipal bond index, and the high-yield bond index.

The important thing to realize about indices in general is that each represents a specific area of the market and, if chosen correctly, can be a reliable source of information when analyzing performance of a portfolio. It is a good idea to select the most applicable index as a benchmark to give an accurate read as to how an investment strategy is performing. Comparing an investment with an irrelevant index provides no additional information about how the portfolio performed. For example, comparing a small-cap strategy with the S&P 500 provides little insight. However, comparing the small-cap strategy with the Russell 2000, the small-cap index, allows the investor to see how well the portfolio is performing relevant to other small companies.

Some of the more important measurements that are helpful to know when investing are the price-to-earnings ratio (P/E), earnings per share (EPS), and price-to-earnings divided by projected earnings growth (PEG).

The P/E is the price of an individual stock, sector, or the overall market, divided by its respective earnings. P/E multiples indicate whether the market is expensive, cheap, or appropriately priced.

The stock market is a forward-looking instrument. Investors are trying to predict what is going to happen, rather than what has already occurred. That's where the P/E ratio can be most helpful. Since the market is forward-looking, it is helpful to look at forward earnings and not trailing earnings. Trailing earnings tell you what occurred, while forecasted forward earnings are a prediction of what is yet to happen.

Sometimes trailing earnings can give the wrong signal, especially during times of extreme change. For instance, during a recession, earnings may have declined significantly but are expected to rebound. For this reason, the expectation of earnings versus the actual earnings offers a more accurate outlook for the future. If the S&P 500 is trading at a P/E multiple of 12, one would want to know if that is a high, moderate, or low multiple to help determine if this is a good time to invest in the market.

For the last 30 years or so, the S&P 500 forward P/E has been at 15. A P/E of 12 indicates that the market is trading at a lower multiple. Therefore, with a multiple of 12, the market would appear to be inexpensive relative to the historical 30-year average.

Forward P/E multiples simply indicate how much investors are currently willing to pay for a year's worth of projected earnings in the future. Strategists often come remarkably close in their predictions of market behavior by considering the P/E multiple, but it's not an exact science.

When evaluating an individual stock, the "E" of the P/E is actually the EPS. EPS is simply the amount of earnings that a company or market made over a specific time period, or is expected to make. Forecasted EPS can be very useful if used as a barometer for bullish or bearish sentiment. However, those investors who use EPS predictions as an exact science are often disappointed. Earnings are typically reported on a quarterly basis, so a great deal of emphasis is placed on the earnings report. Analysts make forecasts of what they believe the earnings will be for specific companies, sectors, and even the entire market. These forecasted earnings are used in determining the forward E of the P/E multiple. When companies report better earnings than were expected, investors typically reward the company by bidding up the stock price. The reverse is true when companies disappoint. As earnings are reported, a company's management also issues future guidance for earnings prospects for the upcoming quarter and sometimes year. Investors listen carefully for signals about a company's outlook for the future.

It's hard enough for an individual company to predict its earnings, much less for an outsider to predict earnings for all 500 components of the S&P 500. However, the numbers can point investors in the right direction if they take projected earnings and the P/E multiples as indications of bullish or bearish sentiment. In other words, a company's earnings predictions can influence the price of a stock, just as the projected multiple that investors are willing to pay for those earnings will also determine the price.

As an example, if a company has an EPS of $1 per year and the P/E is 14, the company's share would trade at $14. Assuming the P/E expanded to 15, the shares would trade at $15. If the P/E contracted to 12, then the shares would trade at $12. Alternatively, assuming earnings of the same company increase to $2 with the P/E remaining at 14, the shares would trade at $28. If earnings dropped to 50 cents, a P/E multiple of 14 would indicate a $7 stock price. In reality, both the earnings and the multiple investors are willing to pay often move simultaneously, which adds complexity in forecasting future stock price.

The stock market of March 2009 provides an example of how P/E multiples can be a useful tool for investors when projecting the overall market. The equity market bottomed out during that month. It was an ugly time. The S&P 500 had peaked in October 2007 and then continued to fall for what seemed like a lifetime, but was actually just about 18 months.

In March 2009, the market appeared to be on the edge of a cliff with another deep canyon to follow. However, the market was trading at about 10 times projected earnings. The S&P dropped down to 666, but earnings were projected to be $65 for the S&P 500 that year. Therefore the S&P was trading at 10 times the EPS projection for the year. This was a bullish indicator because the market appeared to be very inexpensive. The S&P peaked at 1,576 in October 2007, with a forward P/E of 22. Looking back with 20/20 hindsight vision, one can see that the market was too expensive at that time.

Despite the gloom of March 2009, investors who considered the P/E multiple had the benefit of enough knowledge to resist selling out and to stay fully invested in their equity allocation. As the P/E multiple had indicated, March 2009 marked the beginning of a huge turnaround in the market. Investors who let fear take over and sold out at that time missed a significant recovery.

Since the P/E is a ratio of price (the price of the S&P 500 in this example) to earnings (forecasted earnings in this example), there are times when the multiple may stay static while both underlying parts are moving. This is what happened for over two years following the market bottom in 2009. The market doubled in that time, but earnings steadily increased as well. Therefore the overall P/E didn't change as significantly as one might expect, because earnings expectations moved up over the same time.

Putting this in the context of wine, the winemaker is looking for the best spot to plant a vineyard. Just as the winemaker does not plant in areas where temperatures average over 100 in the summer, or average in the 30s during the winter, investors are wise to make certain they are not investing in areas of extreme, as well. The difference with investing, however, is that when you are buying, you would like to pay as low of a multiple as possible, because that means you're paying a lower price for the company's earnings. When selling, you are happy to have high multiples, because that means others are willing to pay you more for the company's earnings power, and this results in higher prices for your holdings.

It's important for investors to remember that P/E multiples vary from market to market, sector to sector, and stock to stock. Faster-growing sectors and companies can command higher multiples. Think of investing as buying a future stream of earnings or cash flow. One is willing to pay more for shares of a company whose earnings are increasing more significantly than another company growing their earnings at a slower rate.

Larry Montclair compared the notion of differentiating growth and value companies to the value of different farming properties. Vineyard owners are willing to pay more for land that offers greater wine production—both in volume and quality—than for land that is not as fruitful.

"Once when I was visiting with my brother about this, he pointed out that comparing different vineyard properties is like comparing the value of different stocks," Larry said, as the tour left the vineyard and headed toward the fermentation warehouse. "He called it the PEG ratio."

Investors are willing to pay more for growth companies—those that are increasing their earnings quickly—because this makes the company more valuable. Investors are not willing to pay as much for value companies because their earnings are not increasing as quickly, even though they may have other positive attributes, such as high dividends. This begs the question: How does one evaluate growth companies in comparison to value companies? Is there a way to compare these two types of companies with one another? The answer is found with another ratio called PEG—P/E to growth—which attempts to provide the investor with a way to compare apples to apples, and apples to oranges.

PEG ratios are a good way to analyze companies with different growth rates. The PEG ratio is derived by taking the forecasted P/E and dividing it by the forecasted earnings growth rate over the next three to five years. PEG ratios below 1 are typically believed to be inexpensive. A PEG of 1 or less indicates that the P/E is at the same level or lower than the expected growth rate of earnings for the company, sector, or index—whichever one is analyzing. Keep in mind that some industries tend to trade at higher PEG ratios than others.

The wine analogy hit home for Rich. He had wondered why some markets, sectors, and companies—such as the technology sector— trade so much more or less than others. If one sector grows at a much faster rate, remembering that this growth is a predictor of future profits, then one is willing to pay more for that holding over something growing at a slower rate.

Considering this, one would expect tech companies to trade at higher multiples than utility companies. However, occasionally investors misprice a market, sector, or individual stock. This provides a savvy investor an opportunity to take advantage of the mispricing, because stocks are unlikely to stay under- or overvalued for long. For example, a technology company may be trading at a P/E multiple of 50, and a utility company may be trading at a multiple of 10. At first glance, one would believe that the utility company is much less expensive than the tech company. However, the tech company has a projected annual earnings growth rate of 50 percent over the next three years while the utility company has a projected annual growth rate of 2 percent over the next three years. By calculating the PEG ratio, we see that the tech company has a PEG ratio of 1, whereas the utility company has a PEG ratio of 5. In this example, on a PEG basis, the tech company is much more attractively priced to a potential buyer than the utility company, all else remaining equal.

As Larry compared farmland to PEG ratios, Rich's mind was starting to spin. The discussion had helped him to understand several basic mechanics of investing: P/E multiples, the importance of predictions, why some investments traded more richly than others, and the basic difference between value investing and growth.

"Wow," Rich said. "The more I start to understand about the stock market, the more I realize the complexity of what I don't understand."

"It's true," Larry said. "My mind has covered a lot of ground in my years here on the vineyard. There's nothing like working with your hands for hours at a time to allow your mind to wander."

Larry mentioned another wine analogy: A grape farmer will look at the sand-to-clay ratio of his soil and the soil's acidity to figure out whether it needs to be fertilized to grow better wine grapes. Once the grapevines are growing, a farmer can actually position the blossoms to make sure they're getting the optimal sun exposure to grow the best fruit. Similarly, an investor can make nuanced changes to his asset allocation, such as under- or overweighting particular asset classes, to reduce exposure to troublesome trends and take advantage of positive ones.

Larry's analogies continued with the winemaking process. He pointed out that different wineries ferment their wine in different types of vessels, ranging from oak barrels to stainless steel, concrete, or plastic. The different materials impart different flavors on the drink. Similarly, an investor must choose the best "vessel" for his investments. Those could include exchange-traded funds, mutual funds, unit investment trusts, variable annuities, structured products, limited partnerships, individual holdings, separately managed accounts, or alternative investments.

Exchange traded funds (ETFs) are becoming ubiquitous and typically represent a specific index of the equity, bond, or commodity markets. These prolific vehicles are traded similarly to stocks and have very low management costs associated with them. Although the types of ETFs are ever increasing, one typically expects index-like returns when using an ETF. Note that some ETFs experience tracking error, the difference in return from the ETF and the underlying benchmark. ETFs are appropriate for fee-sensitive investors who want to achieve index returns minus the small management fees.

Mutual funds are investment vehicles in which investors pool their assets in a comingled fund and give discretion to portfolio managers to make investments on their behalf. They are typically diversified and offer professional management and a track record. They are characterized as either closed-end or open-end. Closed-end funds are similar to ETFs in that they trade on a stock exchange, whereas open-end funds are created as investors invest money into the fund. The portfolio managers add to their holdings as there are positive inflows of cash. When redemptions occur, the portfolio managers may need to liquidate holdings to match the redemptions.

Variable annuities, like mutual funds, are typically diversified comingled investments run by professional portfolio managers. They are unique in that there is insurance built into them that offers a potential safety net in terms of principal protection, often at death, or guaranteed income during one's life. Because they have an element of insurance built into them, they are tax-deferred and can be attractive to certain investors, especially those who are more risk-averse and would like a type of guarantee on their investments by the insurance company. Obviously, the insurance comes with a cost so variable annuities are typically more expensive than open-end mutual funds.

Unit investment trusts (UITs) are also similar to mutual funds in that they are typically diversified vehicles with the underlying investments made according to a portfolio manager, or due to a selection process using a specific strategy such as a quantitative model. UITs are different in that they have a defined maturity, and the underlying investments within the UIT are static, meaning the UIT holds the same underlying securities until the UIT matures.

Structured products are typically a form of derivatives because they normally use underlying holdings to determine their performance. They are becoming increasingly prevalent as investment alternatives. These vehicles are typically designed to enhance performance, reduce risk, or create a yield based on another investment. Investment banks can create structured products upon request to meet a particular investment outlook. Be aware that most structured products are established in a way that the creditworthiness of the issuer can determine whether the structured product will ultimately pay out. In other words, if the issuer goes under, as Lehman Brothers did in 2008, then those structured products are at the mercy of the bankruptcy judge to see if there is any residual value for the investment.

Limited partnerships are investment vehicles that limit liability to investors and place liability on the general partner who manages the investment. They come in multiple styles and offer various strategies. One common form of these is a master limited partnership (MLP). MLPs have a special treatment regarding taxes, and often part of the dividend received from these vehicles is treated as return of principal. This offers tax deferral, and the return of principal is typically deducted from the original cost basis, therefore reducing the investor's cost of purchase by the return of principal. Therefore, when an investor liquidates the MLP, the investor may owe capital gains taxes from the reduced basis versus the sales price. At least, the amount owed is treated as a capital gain or loss and not as ordinary income. MLPs and other limited partnerships often issue K-1s for tax reporting in lieu of 1099s. Often MLPs can cause tax problems if bought within a tax-deferred account. Therefore, MLP holders need to take this into consideration when investing in these vehicles.

Separately managed accounts (SMAs) are investment vehicles that offer diversified portfolios, professional management, and segregated assets. They are similar to mutual funds, but the assets are not comingled with other investors. This is a significant difference from a mutual fund, because the cost basis on the holdings within the portfolio is specific to each investor within the SMA. Having segregated holdings is also an advantage when other investors owning similar strategies decide to add money or take distributions. Since the SMA is not comingled, the SMA holders needn't worry about other investors' investing or withdrawing at inappropriate times. Not only can this be an advantage from an investment standpoint, but possibly from a tax standpoint as well, since other investors' activities take place within their respective portfolios and don't impact those wishing to stay invested.

Alternative investments basically include virtually everything else. Often, alternatives specifically refer to hedge funds, private equity funds, real estate funds, and sometimes commodity funds such as futures strategies. There are numerous types of alternative investments. The attraction to these is often due to many of the strategies having low correlations to traditional long strategies. Alternative investments often have limited liquidity, higher fees, and less disclosure. They are typically designed for higher-net-worth investors and can be appropriate for some investors.

"So, there are many choices," Larry said. "There are all types of companies to invest in and all types of investment vehicles to consider. No one particular way will ever be proven the best way. It's a matter of following sound principles and tinkering around the edges to find the most reliable strategy for your specific needs."

Each portfolio is unique, just like each investor is unique, with his or her own goals, objectives, time horizon, risk tolerance, and cash flow needs.

By then, the tour had wrapped up and Larry was pouring a few tastes for his guests back at the tasting room. Rich marveled at how much he had learned about winemaking over the previous two days. The locals made it seem pretty straightforward, but he also understood that the great wineries learned and adapted as they moved forward. He felt that he and Peg could do the same when it came to building their new investment plan.

"I hope you enjoyed the tour," Larry said. "I know you'll manage your transition just fine. You're obviously giving it serious thought, and that's the key to success."

"Thanks very much," Rich said. "That is encouraging to hear."

"Do you have a wine cellar?" Larry asked.

"We do, but there's not much to it," Peg replied.

Larry handed them a bottle of Frais Valley Merlot. "Now you'll have the finest cellar in all of Texas," he said with a smile.

"And speaking of wine cellars, they're also comparable to investment portfolios," Larry said. "Each wine collector's cellar reflects his taste, income, and time. Most want to have a nice bottle of wine for next week's dinner as well as extra-special bottles for special occasions. I've seen wine collectors who put their cellars together logically and methodically, while others stock up on a haphazard basis. In my opinion, it's the collectors who take a little time and learn the basics who really enjoy collecting over the long term. This is very similar to investors: Some seem to just hold a random assortment of securities, while others seem to base their decisions on reason. From our conversation today, I'd say you fall into the reason camp, Rich. Here's to years of success and enjoyment from your cellar, and from your portfolio."

Chapter 8

The Marathon Runner and Time Horizon

Winter flew by for the Vivas, as Rich settled into a retirement routine and tried to keep busy. He exercised on a daily basis at the gym at the Houstonian, read books he'd been meaning to open for years, and paid visits to his old friends. Rich even joined the board of directors for the Association of Independent Oilfield Service Companies, the trade group he had chaired earlier in his career. The job required only a few hours of work per month. Rich enjoyed the work, especially because it provided a way to keep in touch with the industry.

The holidays were a blur of activity with family and friends. The only downside was that Rich and Peg's son, Patrick, had declined to visit for the holiday, opting instead to experience Christmas in Paris. The Vivas tried to convince their son to come to Houston, but he'd become enamored of the French lifestyle and was determined to spend the season there.

Rich had continued to work on developing his financial plan, although he worked on it in fits and starts. The process nagged at him and tended to create stress. He thought about investment concepts quite frequently, read investing guidebooks, and contemplated his goals and objectives. He and Peg had set a goal of finalizing their plan by the summer. Rich liked having time to consider his options, but the process weighed on him despite the general relaxation of retirement.

By the third month of retirement, Rich had grown accustomed to the new pace of his life. It was the first time in his adult life that he'd been able to completely leave his work behind. ACS was no longer Rich's concern, although, as Peg had pointed out, Rich had managed to replace his business preoccupation by means of fretting over their financial future. Still, retirement gave both of them a sense of freedom and liberty that felt new and different in this phase of their lives.

The Vivas' next big trip was set for April. They arranged to travel to Boston to see their daughter, Laura, run in the Boston Marathon. The trip snuck up sooner than expected, but the Vivas were ready to hit the road again. They stuffed their winter clothes into their baggage just in case. It had been a warm winter in Houston, and their heavy coats and sweaters hadn't seen much use that year.

Laura's participation in the Boston Marathon was a big accomplishment, and her parents felt they should travel to New England to watch and support her. Being a mom, Peg also felt somebody had to be there in case something went wrong. At the first mention of being there for Laura, Rich quickly agreed. Like most parents, the two of them loved their children more than life itself.

Laura, 25, had run cross-country in high school, but didn't run competitively in college. The year before, she and a friend had decided to run the Austin Marathon. Laura threw herself into the training and regained some of her speed from her days as a cross-country runner. On race day, she surprised herself and everybody else with a really fast time—3:32—that qualified her for the Boston Marathon. Laura had taken a break after the Austin Marathon, but then started her training hard again in the months leading up to Boston. She joined Houston Fit, a training team with a coach, to help her prepare for the race.

The Vivas were also excited about doing some sightseeing in Boston. They'd built a couple extra days into their trip to spend touring the various attractions—the university campuses, Boston Common, and the Freedom Trail.

Rich, Peg, and Laura arrived in Boston on a Saturday in mid-April, two days before the Monday race. They had reservations at the Four Seasons directly across from the Public Garden. It was fun to see the swan boats at the garden. They had read *Make Way for Ducklings*, about the ducks that made Public Garden their home, so many times when the kids were younger that they still could recite parts of the book by memory. The three spent the remaining time on Saturday touring Boston and shopping at Faneuil Hall. For dinner, they went to The Daily Catch on Hanover. "Cozy" would be an understatement for the 360-square-foot restaurant with a kitchen that opens to a tiny dining room with only five tables and a capacity of 20 people. The place made Jonathan's The Rub, one of their favorite neighborhood restaurants in Houston, seem huge.

On Sunday afternoon, Rich and Laura went over to the John B. Hynes Convention Center to pick up Laura's race bib and runner's packet, while Peg spent some time window-shopping on Boylston Street. Excitement was building as runners from around the country and the world were milling around the convention center. The next day's race was at the forefront of everyone's mind. The runners were preoccupied with visualizing the race—their time, energy, pace, and endurance. For the spectators, parking, road closures, transportation, and keeping warm were the primary topics of concern.

Even Rich was getting caught up in the excitement. For the first time in a long time he was focused more on Laura and her soon-to-be accomplishment than on his financial plan, and how those decisions would impact the remainder of his and Peg's lives. Over the years, Rich had found that his intense level of focus was what drove him to success. It was good to leave it behind for a while and to focus on his daughter. There would be time in the future to worry about finances.

After getting their fill of everything regarding the marathon, Rich and Laura met Peg at an Italian restaurant for a carbohydrate-loading dinner, a tradition of many distance runners. The three met at L'Osteria on Salem Street in Boston's Little Italy in the North End. The small, intimate restaurant was perfect and was exactly as they had pictured. Laura was able to get the carbs she needed, and although Rich and Peg didn't particularly need carbs, they decided to join in the fun anyway.

"So, what's the plan for your big run tomorrow, Laura?" Peg asked over dinner.

"My first goal is to complete the 26.2 miles," said Laura.

"That seems really ambitious," Rich chided. He knew Laura surely had a more challenging goal for herself. "Mom and I didn't come all this way just to see you finish."

"All right, my *real* plan is to not only finish but to set a personal best and avoid injury," Laura said.

The year before, Laura had finished the Austin Marathon in 3:32. She wanted to shave 10 minutes off her time in the Boston race. That meant she would need to average 7 minutes and 42.6 seconds per mile. In Austin, she had averaged 8 minutes and 5.05 seconds per mile.

"Ten minutes may not sound like a big difference, but it's actually about 23 seconds per mile," Laura said.

"That's my girl," Rich boasted. "This is exactly why you will go far in life, Laura! You have that Viva laser focus and determination needed to succeed in life. I have no doubt you will do great."

"As long as you don't get hurt and have fun along the way, we will be proud of you, Laura," Peg added. "We are proud of you no matter what."

"You can do it; I know you can. In fact, I believe you can do anything you set your mind to," Rich said. "You've trained hard, you're smart, and you have experience. I have complete confidence in you. Tomorrow night Mom and I plan to take you to Number 9 Park to celebrate your accomplishment! It's right across the park from the hotel, so it will be easy to get to after the race."

"The concierge tells us it's the best in Boston, and only steps from the State House. I think they pulled some strings to get us in," Peg said.

"Sounds good to me," Laura said. "But it's hard for me to think about tomorrow night's dinner when I've got 26 miles to run before then. Do you think we can get back to the hotel soon so I can try to get to sleep before 10?"

"Of course, Laura. Waiter, may we have our check please? Our daughter needs to get some rest tonight before she finishes the Boston Marathon in record time tomorrow," Rich boisterously said, loud enough for the surrounding tables to hear. He didn't realize that many of the lean, athletic patrons at surrounding tables were also getting ready for tomorrow's big day.

The next morning, Rich and Peg positioned themselves near the middle of the course, at around mile 14 in Wellesley along Washington Street. The girls of Wellesley College could be heard from miles around as they cheered along the marathoners.

The Vivas thought it would be the perfect spot to cheer Laura and still have time to make it to the finish to celebrate. It wasn't long before they wished they had brought earplugs to help drown out the constant roar of the spirited spectators. There were thousands of onlookers crowded onto the streets and sidewalks. Rich and Peg bided their time as a river of runners passed by en route to the finish.

The weather wasn't helping anybody. It was rainy, cold, and windy—the kind of weather that had plagued Boston's inhabitants since the city's founding. The Vivas ducked in and out of White Mountain Creamery for shelter and warm drinks. The shop was packed with other shivering spectators taking cover from the elements. Glen, the owner of the ice cream shop, told Rich the marathon was always their busiest day of the year. The only difference was some years they sold more ice cream, while others it was coffee.

To follow Laura's progress in the race, the Vivas had signed up to get text messages updating Laura's location and pace. Laura's progress was sporadic. The limited information in the text messages indicated that her pace was inconsistent. Some of the mileage markers didn't pick up a reading on her.

"I hope she's doing okay," Peg said as she sipped her second cup of coffee from the Creamery.

"This weather isn't helping much," Rich said. "I didn't ask her about her clothes. I hope she brought something warm."

"She brought clothes for any kind of weather," Peg said. "Her plan was to bring multiple layers of old sweats and discard them early in the race as she got warm. I read that the Boston Marathon donates all the clothing found along the route to the Big Brothers Big Sisters organization."

"At this point, I'd rather be running a marathon than standing around in this weather," Rich said, and Peg agreed.

The first text alert, at the 10-kilometer marker, indicated that Laura was going a bit slower than her projected pace. It read 53:05, or about 8:32 minutes per mile. At that pace, she would complete the marathon in 3:44—slower than she had discussed over dinner the night before.

Rich and Peg waited in anticipation and chuckled about the Wellesley girls' enthusiasm. "If this group doesn't motivate you, I don't know if anything could," Rich said.

For Laura, the race wasn't going as she had planned. She knew her timing was off. The first mile was crowded and was naturally slower due to the sheer volume of people. At the same time, the excitement was causing many of the runners to run a bit faster than originally planned. This was common even with this elite group.

Laura was in control and would not fall into the trap of starting out too fast and "bonking" later in the race. She concentrated on slowing her pace in order to finish strong. However, at about mile 5, she realized she had held back too much and her time was not close to her goal. She picked up her pace, but she ended up overcompensating.

As Laura approached the midway mark she could hear the roar of the Wellesley girls. She knew she would see her mom and dad shortly. Without thinking it through, she let her emotions drive her forward and at the halfway mark her watch read 1:35; she had made up for the slower pace of the first 5 miles of the race.

As Laura was approaching Rich and Peg, they received a text update that said Laura had finished half the race in 1 hour and 35 minutes, with an average mile time of 7:15.

"Could this be accurate?" Peg questioned.

Before long it was confirmed, as they saw Laura with their own eyes.

"How could she have made up so much time between the 10 K and the half?" Rich asked. "I just don't get it. I bet the first reading was off."

In fact, neither the first nor the second reading was wrong. Laura had run at a pace of 6:05 per mile between the 6.2-mile point and the halfway mark of 13.1 miles. Laura's drive and determination drove her to run at an unsustainable pace during the second quarter of the race, a pace she had never run before other than in short sprints.

Rich and Peg cheered as Laura ran by. Laura gave them a thumbs-up sign and looked at them with a winded smile.

"I knew she would do it. Look at her. She's going to break her goal and then some," Rich said proudly.

The parents had no time to waste—especially if they were to make it to the finish area to meet Laura after the race. They hurriedly left to their rental car to make it toward Boston. Rich was accustomed to battling traffic from his commute over the years, and Peg navigated the street closures. The two made a good team. As they drove into Boston, their worries of missing Laura at the finish gave way to worrying if she would even finish. At least an hour had passed since the midway point, and they hadn't received a text update since then.

"Do you think there's something wrong with the texting? They had problems with this a few years ago," Rich complained.

The Vivas were driving in downtown Boston, nearing the finishing line, when they received the 30-kilometer alert, or three quarters through the race. Laura's pace had dropped substantially. This time the alert read 3:34. She had finished the Austin Marathon in about that time, but now she still had 10 kilometers to run.

It was a confusing turn of events. "What's going on? Could this even be accurate?" Peg said.

Peg and Rich waited next to the "V" sign in the family waiting area along St. James Avenue. It felt like hours passed, especially in the cold Boston weather. They were thrilled and relieved to see Laura when she finally arrived. But she didn't look good. She looked cold and exhausted. She was stiff and bent over as she hobbled up to them, shivering under her thermal blanket. Most of the runners looked tired, but Rich thought Laura looked particularly worn out.

"Congratulations!" Peg said as she and Rich gave Laura a hug. "We knew you could do it."

They didn't mention the fact that Laura had missed her goal by over an hour.

Laura responded with a tired and annoyed look. She was in no mood to talk.

They all walked quietly back to the car. Back at the hotel, Rich and Peg gave Laura the space she needed. She went through her post-race recovery routine that she'd learned in her running class: first, a hot shower to get warm, then a cool bath to prevent cramps, followed by several bottles of water to prevent dehydration. An hour or so later, Laura arrived at the adjoining room looking sullen and dressed in jeans and a sweater.

"I hope Number 9 Park will take me looking like this tonight. I know you two were really looking forward to it," Laura said somewhat pathetically.

"We don't have to go to the restaurant," Peg said. "We should have thought that you might be a little tired and not in the mood for going out."

"It's okay," Laura said. "I want to go eat. I just can't believe how badly the race went.

"It's a long story. I'll lay it all out when we get to the restaurant."

The three walked silently across the park and found the restaurant only steps from the golden-domed State House. The Vivas already knew Laura's time was bad, based on the race text message updates. It had taken Laura 4:47 to finish the race, a full hour and 27 minutes behind her goal of 3:20.

As soon as they were seated, Rich asked, "So what happened? It seemed like your pace went up and down throughout the race."

"No kidding," Laura said. "My pace was all over the place. I never really felt comfortable. There were just too many problems."

She explained how the race unraveled for her.

"It all happened so quickly, even though it took me almost five hours to complete the race. Most of it is a blur," Laura said.

She recalled how she got off the bus in Hopkinton, and found the Porta Potty lines and then her corral to begin the race.

When the starter's pistol fired, the crowd of runners lurched forward. The first mile was super-crowded. Laura was pumped with excitement, and the course started downhill, both of which contributed to a faster pace. But the crowded conditions slowed everybody down. Laura was trying to pace herself as her running coach had instructed her, but she found it difficult given the competing factors of the crowd versus the excitement and downhill slope.

"Looking back on it, I think I overcompensated and went too slow. I never seemed to be able to just run freely like I did in Austin. Maybe I thought about it too much."

At about mile 5, Laura realized she was falling behind her benchmark targets and decided to speed up to make up time. But she overcompensated again, setting an unsustainable pace.

"I remember when I started feeling like I was overexerting myself," she recalled. "I had just run by the screaming girls at Wellesley College and I was pumped. Then I looked up and I was at mile 13, fairly close to the halfway marker. After my pathetic first five miles, I was almost shocked to see that I was back on track to hit my goal. Then I saw the two of you, standing there cheering me on, and I really wanted to hit my goal like we talked about at dinner last night. At that point I was thinking I could overcome the sporadic pace and make my target time."

Laura said she kept monitoring her watch, doing math in her head, and trying to figure out where she had gone wrong.

That's when events took a turn for the worse. Shortly after Laura ran past her parents in Wellesley, an older man running a few yards ahead of Laura suddenly collapsed.

"He fell and banged his face on the pavement," Laura recalled. "I stopped and saw blood running out of his mouth and a bunch of teeth scattered on the asphalt. The guy was about 60 years old. I almost puked on the spot."

The man was unconscious. Laura ran to the nearest police officer, who radioed for the paramedics. Police officers were tending to the man, but Laura didn't feel like she could abandon him until the paramedics arrived, which was about two minutes later.

"After the EMS got there, I figured I should get running again," Laura explained. "At that point, I was pretty freaked out. I wasn't sure if that guy was even going to survive.

"So I pushed off to get going again and felt my left calf seize up."

It was a painful muscle cramp. Laura hobbled to the side of the course to stretch and drink water.

"So now I'm stuck there trying to loosen up my calf. It's freezing cold, which doesn't help. And I'm watching the EMS load the old guy onto an ambulance on a stretcher."

Laura said she tried not to look at the timer on her watch, but she glanced down and saw the minutes ticking away.

"I seriously thought about quitting at that point, because I knew my time was shot. There was no way I was going to even match my Austin time, much less beat it."

That's when it started to rain. It was a cold, gusty rain—the messy weather that Peg and Rich had stood in for hours.

"If I had been running steadily, I don't think the cold rain would have bothered me, but because I was stopped, I got really cold. I was shivering and trying to warm up."

Laura kept running, but she'd lost her spirit for the race. Her time was shot, her calf was bothering her, she still felt queasy about the fallen runner, and now she was shivering in the cold rain. She was then in Newton, home of the infamous Heartbreak Hill. Even the slightest hill can seem like a mountain after running 20 miles, especially to someone used to the flat streets of Houston. Laura struggled up the hills and finished the race, forcing herself through the last 10 miles. But she considered it a failure to meet her goal.

"I didn't really have any fun for the rest of the race," Laura said. "It was just a matter of getting to the finish. I just didn't want to drop out of the race."

Laura's inconsistent pace and depressed look at the finish made more sense to Rich and Peg.

"Well, I think it's really amazing that you finished considering all of that," Peg said. "I'm really proud of you."

Laura nodded and grinned. "Yeah, could you imagine how upset I would be if I didn't finish? The weird part is that I got totally rattled, and that didn't happen in Austin. I'm not exactly sure where I got off track. In the end, I think I was more upset by my problems setting a pace than by the weather or the old guy who collapsed."

"So do you think you'll run another one?" Rich asked.

"Oh yes," Laura said. "Not right away. I'm going to take a nice long break. But I can't let the taste of today be my final experience running a marathon."

"That's my girl," Rich said with a big smile.

As they dined, Rich's mind wandered to a thought he'd been having during the long, cold hours of watching the race. The whole idea of preparation and pacing for a marathon reminded him of his development of an investment plan.

Ernie, Rich's old friend and fishing partner from the Jackson Hole trip, had talked about the concept of a time horizon, or the length of time an investor has to invest his money and how that affects his strategy.

Rich was having a hard time concentrating on Peg and Laura's conversation about the pending marriage of an acquaintance, so he seized on a lull in the conversation to bring up his idea.

"You probably didn't think about how your problems setting a pace were similar to mismanaging cash flow," Rich said to Laura.

Laura squinted at her father in confusion. Peg rolled her eyes.

"Hear me out," Rich said. "By starting too slow and then over-compensating by going too fast, you mismanaged your time."

"I already know that," Laura said.

"But there's a financial lesson here," Rich said. "That's kind of like an investor who is reliant on cash flow for his expenses. The investor needs to ration his money and avoid the temptation to spend it too fast. Because what if there's a crisis, and you need more than what you planned on?

"Then you could be in trouble, in the same way you suddenly found yourself dealing with the injured runner. You didn't have the time or energy to deal with the crisis, but you felt you had no choice.

"At the same time, you don't want to run so slow that you finish the race wishing that you'd given more. That's like an investor who is so worried about saving for the future that he doesn't enjoy himself and grows too old to actually enjoy his money."

Peg interjected. "You see, Laura, ever since your dad sold ACS he's been worrying about our financial situation. Not that there's much to worry about. We're developing a financial plan to invest our money and make the most of the profits from the business sale. I've been having a lot of conversations like this with your dad recently."

She turned to Rich. "So you're comparing time horizon to a marathon?"

"I guess so," Rich said. "And the idea that you've got to pace yourself in your investment plan, just like a marathon runner sets a pace. Can you imagine how depressing it must be to find yourself in the golden years realizing too late that you spent too much early on, not saving enough or investing correctly?

"It's not just for your mom and me, Laura. Our goal is to leave something for you and Patrick, as well as to some of our favorite organizations that could use a little help—like the foundation at church and other worthy charities," Rich added.

Laura considered her father's point.

"I've found that running a marathon is 90 percent willpower and 10 percent physical strength," she said. "However, running is definitely physical; just ask the runners who hit the wall. I've seen it in both marathons I've run. People who start out too fast and end up failing."

"That's the same as someone spending too much money and depleting their nest egg," Rich replied. "Once it's gone, it's awfully hard making it back. Just ask all the lottery winners who spend their money like it grows on trees. All too often they end up broke with nothing but a few good memories and lots of heartache."

Rich took a sip of Meritage and thought about the analogy.

"And then there's the issue of external forces complicating your time horizon," he said. "Like when the injured runner and the weather contributed to the demise of your plan for the race."

In investing, an example of an external issue that could hurt an investor's planning and time horizon would be an outbreak of war in the Middle East, a terrorist attack in the United States, a downgrade of sovereign debt, or any number of major events. During times of uncertainty, the stock market usually drops as investors worry about economic stability.

An investor needs his cash flow—the money he periodically pulls from his earnings to cover living expenses—to be in good shape. Otherwise, he might have to cash out part of his portfolio when the market is low. That's the worst option, because the investor may be getting much less than he would have in a better market when his holdings were more valuable.

"When the cold rain started during the race, your thoughts and energy had to shift to keeping warm and motivated," Rich said to Laura. "If you had been on pace when those challenges occurred, it's more likely you would have had an easier time maintaining your composure and making a strong finish."

"Yes, but I finished the race," Laura said defensively.

"Of course, and that's amazing, considering the difficulty and the obstacles," Rich said. "But bear with me here for a second. You didn't reach the time goal you had set for yourself. It's like an investor who mismanages his time horizon and has to cash out part of his portfolio at the wrong time, thereby negatively affecting his portfolio for the long term."

The time horizon planning concept is really about having the cash flow there when you need it. If you consider your time horizon wisely and separate your cash flow out of your portfolio, you're much more likely to have a good experience over the long term (Exhibit 8.1).

"He's been acting like this a lot?" Laura asked her mother.

They were enjoying dessert and after-dinner coffee. All three were having decaf, but after Laura's day, she could have a double espresso and still find herself asleep as soon as her head hit the pillow.

"Yes, but it's not as crazy as it may sound," Peg responded. "Now that he doesn't have ACS to worry about, his mind seems to be pre-occupied with financial planning."

"I fear your mom thinks I'm turning into my old friend Fred Burdon, who is a nervous wreck regarding investments. In reality, I'm trying to avoid being like him. I figure if I develop a well-thought-out plan, just as you did to compete in this race, then one day I can simply enjoy the fruits of my labor without worrying so much," Rich said.

The last thing he wanted was to be like Fred Burdon. "I don't want to drive myself or you guys crazy, but there's a lot to think about," he added.

"Dad, do you remember when I first decided to run the marathon and you gave me some advice?" Laura remarked. "You recommended that if I decided to do it, then I needed to totally commit to it—practice, join a running group, get some coaching.

The longer you hold stocks,
the less the likelihood of loss and surer the likelihood of gain

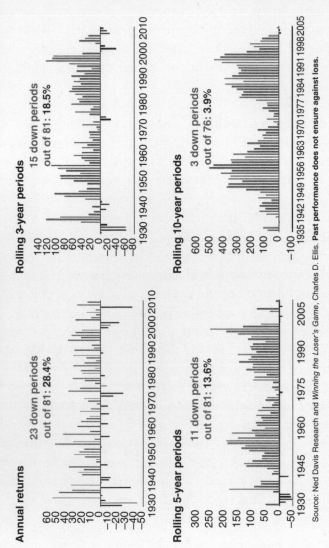

Annual returns

23 down periods
out of 81: **28.4%**

Rolling 3-year periods

15 down periods
out of 81: **18.5%**

Rolling 5-year periods

11 down periods
out of 81: **13.6%**

Rolling 10-year periods

3 down periods
out of 76: **3.9%**

Source: Ned Davis Research and *Winning the Loser's Game*, Charles D. Ellis. **Past performance does not ensure against loss.**

Exhibit 8.1 Historically, on an annual basis, 28 percent of the time the equity market has been negative. However, the number of negative occurrences drops by half when viewing negative down periods over five-year intervals. For those with a 10-year investment horizon, historically the domestic equity market has been down less than 4 percent of rolling 10-year periods. The more time that an investor has to invest, the more likely the investor will experience a positive return.

"You basically said that I should make the sacrifices necessary to achieve my goal," Laura added. "That way, I could enjoy myself along the way because I had prepared properly."

"Sure I remember," Rich responded. "Life is too short to go around all stressed without being able to enjoy the roses along the way."

"I've been so busy training, I haven't been around you as much as I would like," Laura said. "But it seems like you need to take your own advice. You decided to sell the company. Now you're going through a big adjustment and learning how to tackle the next stage of life. Just make certain you enjoy the journey along the way. I love you guys and I want you to be around for a long time. Try not to worry so much. Okay?" Laura said.

At that moment, Peg and Rich realized their little girl had maturity and wisdom beyond her years. They couldn't have been prouder of the woman she had become.

Rich's stress level immediately dropped a notch or two. All the money was a good thing, he thought, and he and Peg would come up with a plan that was right for their family and their needs.

Rich had learned a lot during their short trip to Boston. First, Laura's marathon experience drove home the point that time horizon is an important factor in determining his cash flow needs. Second, he was reminded that the money from the business sale was a blessing. It didn't need to be a burden to develop a plan, and, if done right, perhaps he could even enjoy the journey along the way. Third, the time with Laura confirmed what he had always known: He and Peg were two extremely fortunate parents.

Chapter 9

Cash Flow

The following morning, Rich and Peg left the hotel for the airport while Laura slept in, since her flight wasn't scheduled to depart until later in the afternoon. There had been some miscommunication between Laura and her parents, and Peg felt badly that they were leaving early without her, but Laura didn't seem to be concerned.

During the cab ride to Logan International Airport, Rich struck up a conversation with the driver. Peg often accused Rich of never knowing a stranger, and once again he proved her correct. Rich had a knack for easily empathizing with those around him and was curious to learn their stories. He especially enjoyed conversing with those who had a strong work ethic.

The driver, Habib, pointed out city landmarks and other points of interest. Rich marveled once again at Boston's rich history. He took the opportunity to ask the driver about his own background. Habib, like so many cabbies in other big cities, had fled his homeland to escape something—perhaps an oppressive regime, abject poverty, a lack of opportunity, or some combination of the three. It often amazed Rich to learn of the immigrants' plight and their desire for a better life.

Over the years of riding to and from airports in taxis, Rich enjoyed learning about the drivers who seemed to have remarkably similar experiences. It amazed Rich how brave people like Habib would have to be to leave everything behind to seek a better life. All were here to find something better in the land of opportunity, the United States of America.

As they sped past another intersection, Rich and Peg learned that Habib had moved to Boston 25 years earlier and had been driving a taxi ever since. Habib and his wife had raised three children in Boston, all of whom were being educated there. He was very proud of all of them. The eldest was graduating from college and was starting medical school the next semester. The next oldest, a junior in college, was studying business and planned to become a businessman.

"He tells me one day he will own this cab company," Habib added. "But I hope he goes into a different field."

The youngest was in ninth grade and was planning to become a pop singer. If that didn't work out, she planned to graduate with a fashion design degree and develop her own clothing line. "Only in America," Rich thought.

Rich found it comforting to know that there were still those out there willing to take risks and find success. Habib left his homeland with nothing, found a job in a new country, stuck with it for 25 years, and raised a family. His children would be educated, hardworking taxpayers of the United States.

"If only our own people would realize how great we have it here," Rich thought.

The United States was still the great melting pot. Rich couldn't help but compare himself to Habib and question whether he would have had the guts to leave everything behind to seek fortune across the sea.

Rich also wondered how the driver could toil in his blue-collar job and still find a way to motivate his three children to make something of themselves. It was a question common to all parents, rich or poor, no matter where they lived.

Rich wasn't worried about Laura. She was a go-getter and had her father's drive and focus. But his son, Patrick, seemed to be more like Habib's third child. The difference was that Patrick was already in college, while Habib's daughter's dream was more understandable as a ninth-grader's fantasy.

As they pulled up to Logan International, Peg and Rich wished Habib well.

"Here's a little something to help with all the tuition you're paying," Rich said.

Habib was grateful and jumped out of his seat to help unload their luggage and to shake Rich's hand. It made Rich feel great to think he was helping this man and his family.

Rich and Peg entered the airport and checked in with United for their flight back to Houston. While the Vivas were waiting at the gate, the airline announced that their flight was delayed for at least one hour because of storms in Houston. They wandered over to the United Club, United's reception area for premium passengers, to kill time and drink coffee. Rich's membership in the Continental Airlines President's Club was still in effect from when he had joined during his days of frequent business travel, before Continental merged with United Airlines.

"We should renew our membership to this club, because it's always a nice perk to be able to visit these quiet areas, especially for long waits," Peg said.

"Yeah, they are nice," Rich said. "But we joined based on frequent-flyer benefits. I don't know if we could justify buying a membership without flying that much."

Peg rolled her eyes. "There you go again, Ebenezer," she said. "It seems like we're flying quite a bit.

"I wish Laura was on the same flight as us," she added. "I don't know how I got the times wrong for our flight."

"She'll be fine, Peg. You've booked a lot of flights recently. It's probably not easy keeping up with our new travel itinerary," Rich said.

"I just wish she would have allowed us to have covered her flight. She is so incredibly independent," Peg replied.

"Well, her brother doesn't seem to have a problem with allowing us to pick up his travel costs," Rich said. "I wonder what Habib would do with Patrick."

With that, Peg walked to the nearby bar to order coffee without responding. She, too, was worried about their son, Patrick, but she didn't feel like talking about it then.

Rich relaxed in his armchair and opened up the copy of the *Boston Globe* he'd purchased in the terminal.

Peg returned with the coffee and news from the video board that their flight had been delayed at least another hour. There was nothing to do but grin and bear it. Rich flipped through the newspaper, and Peg read the latest novel by Jeffrey Archer, her favorite author. She had discovered the new release while perusing a Boston bookstore when Rich and Laura were picking up the race packet on Sunday.

About that time Rich noticed a fellow on the neighboring couch, a man about his age, late 50s or early 60s, with gray hair and a big gray mustache. The man's casual attire and New York Yankees cap indicated he was traveling for pleasure. Rich had just read a newspaper story about the Yankees beating the Houston Astros the night before in a rare interleague meeting.

"Congrats to the Yankees, although beating the Astros this year is not much of a feat," Rich said to the man.

The stranger laughed and shrugged. "I'll take any kind of win," he said. "I didn't catch the game. Did you?"

"No," Rich answered. "I just saw the score here in the news-paper. I'm from Houston, so I kind of follow the Astros. It's been getting harder and harder in recent years with the team being so miserable."

The two men introduced themselves.

Tom Pepperdino, 66, was from Cranbury, New Jersey, and had retired four years earlier from his job as an executive at Sun Pharma-ceuticals. He had been in Boston to visit his son, a banker, and was waiting for his flight to Los Angeles to see the Yankees play the Los Angeles Angels of Anaheim.

Tom said he was traveling cross-country to see the Yankees play because he'd never seen a game at the Angels stadium in Anaheim and it was part of his mission to see a game at every ballpark in Major

League Baseball. He'd visited 24 of the 30 stadiums so far, mostly in the East and Midwest. He had checked 20 stadiums off of his list in his four years of retirement.

Tom's story struck a chord with Rich. He was intrigued by Tom's relatively recent retirement and his apparent financial comfort that allowed him to pursue his interests. It was refreshing, and Rich thought maybe he could aspire to do something as carefree someday.

"That's really neat," Rich said. "It sounds like you've been flying all over the country if you've seen 20 stadiums in four seasons."

"Some of them were flights," Tom answered. "A lot of them are within driving distance here on the East Coast, and I took the train to a few games. I definitely flew when I went to the Astros' stadium."

Rich's face brightened. "So you've been to Houston? That's great. We're proud of our ballpark downtown. It's been a nice thing for the city since the Astros moved from the Astrodome to downtown."

"I really liked Enron Field," Tom said with a nod. "That retractable outfield roof was something else."

"Yeah, well, they wouldn't sell any tickets if it was an outdoor field, because it gets so hot," Rich said. "It must have been a while since you've been there, because they took the Enron name off the park, for obvious reasons. Now it's called Minute Maid Park, of all things."

Tom chuckled. "That's right. I'd forgotten about that. I guess it would be tough to leave the Enron name on anything."

Enron was an enormous Houston-based corporation that marketed commodities like electricity and natural gas. It was one of the country's most powerful companies before it collapsed under the weight of an accounting scandal in 2001. The company's bankruptcy was widely felt throughout Houston, especially by the employees who'd been partly compensated with stock in the company.

Rich's company was largely unscathed by the Enron debacle, mainly because he did most of his work with oil and gas companies other than Enron. Rich always felt that had been a brush of good luck. The example of Enron had come to mind when Rich had heard the story of his former high school teacher Judy Kenneth. She and her husband had most of their savings invested in Hatfield Energy Corp. shares when that company went belly-up.

"Just another reminder to diversify," Rich said to Tom.

"Isn't that the truth," Tom said. "I always felt terrible for those people who worked for Enron and had no idea it was a house of cards."

"You can imagine what a big deal that was in Houston," Rich said.

The discussion sent Rich's thoughts wandering. Other than a short reprieve while focusing on Laura during the marathon, his mind had been racing for months with concern over his retirement and financial security. Peg and others had assured Rich that things would turn out okay, yet he never felt at peace with the situation.

Rich's logical side told him that the $12 million he'd profited on the business sale would be more than enough for his family. But he'd seen the market crash before. He knew of the bear market of 1973 to 1974, but since he didn't have much money invested back then, it didn't seem all that bad. The tech bubble that burst in early 2000 and lasted through 2002 had been painful, but nothing like the pain of the October 2007 to March 2009 pullback.

Those 18 months felt like a lifetime of torture for most investors. Rich had lost money in the market, but nothing like the horror stories he'd read of retirees losing their invested savings over a matter of months. Enron was another example of a financial disaster that could really hurt a well-intentioned investor. Swindlers like Bernie Madoff, Allen Stanford, and MF Global didn't help much in giving anyone confidence.

Rich didn't want to pry into Tom's personal business, so he just mentioned that he was six months into his own retirement after selling his oilfield services company. Retirement had been a whirlwind so far, he said, with trips to Wyoming, California, and Boston, as well as the holidays.

"But I've got to tell you," Rich said. "All this travel makes me nervous. It's not like we're shopping for diamonds in Dubai, but I'm not used to spending money when I'm not making it."

Tom smiled and nodded his head in understanding.

"I know where you're coming from," he said. "I was pretty nervous when I retired. I figured I could've worked at least another 10 years, but my wife urged me to quit before it was too late. Now

I'm really happy I decided to retire. I can't imagine going to the office."

"What about the market crash?" Richard asked. "How bad was that for you? I've heard some pretty depressing stories about retirees who took big hits."

"Well, that was definitely stressful," Tom said. "But we were never overly nervous, because we had our cash flow ladder set up to cover our expenses and travel."

Rich had heard about the idea of a cash flow ladder. Basically, it's a financial strategy that calls for setting aside a few years of spending money—rather than investing the money as part of a portfolio—so that investors don't have to rely on their portfolio to generate earnings for living expenses. A cash flow ladder is a safety blanket of sorts. Investors can count on having the cash they need to live on without panicking over every dip or surge in the markets. Periodically, as some parts of the portfolio perform better than others, the cash flow ladder is replenished by harvesting gains from the better-performing strategies and sectors.

Tom continued with his story. He had retired in 2007, when the stock market was good. He had been an active investor over the previous 30 years, but he developed an entirely new investment plan after he retired. Tom and his advisor positioned the new plan for growth, but also placed a greater emphasis on distributing earnings because Tom and his wife were no longer earning income. At his financial advisor's suggestion, Tom and his wife also decided it would be worth keeping some of their savings on the sideline for spending cash—their cash flow ladder.

Tom realized the importance of his own cash flow ladder after watching his older brother's experience. When Tom's brother retired in 2000, the future looked great and the market was riding high. As is the case every time the market gets high, most investors were very optimistic. Tom's brother's portfolio was producing good returns, so he put almost all of his money into his investment portfolio and lived on capital gains and dividend payments. Like many other investors at that time, Tom's brother concentrated his portfolio in the technology sector—the king of the surge. At the time, the late 1990s and beginning of 2000, investors' returns were minimal if technology wasn't a considerable part of their portfolio. The period was later referred to as the tech bubble.

The plan worked for a while, but didn't turn out well in the end. In March 2000, the S&P 500 peaked at 1,552, the tech bubble burst, and the S&P dropped by half before hitting a low of 768 in October 2002. In investing, the longer investors stay in the market, the more value their investments typically accumulate. Similarly, the sequence of returns is vitally important during the early stages of retirement—especially without a cash flow ladder. When the market crashed, Tom's brother's portfolio dropped in value and stopped producing returns. He had to cash out part of his portfolio when it was undervalued just to have money to cover basic expenses. This had a compounding effect, because not only did he sell at a low point and therefore with less money, he also didn't have as much in the market as it started its recovery. His investment experience was not good.

Tom was not going to make the same mistake his brother had made. To start, Tom and his wife sat down to figure out how much they could live on per year. They'd been told by their financial advisor that they had enough money to withdraw $200,000 a year from their portfolio for living expenses. But they wanted to be slightly conservative and decided on a figure of $180,000: $150,000 for general living expenses and $30,000 for travel. So they took $720,000—four years worth of cash flow—out of their potential investment funds and set it aside.

The first $180,000, they left in cash for year one. Then they bought three certificates of deposit (CDs) for the remaining three years. They put $180,000 in a one-year CD for the second year of the ladder, $180,000 in a two-year CD for the third year, and $180,000 in a three-year CD for the fourth year.

"At first, it was difficult to watch so much of our cash sitting in short- and medium-term fixed-income assets, making virtually nothing. In fact, if you look at the real return after inflation, some of it may be generating a slight loss," Tom said. "But then my wife reminded me of my brother's first few years of retirement, and we decided to play it safe with the cash flow ladder."

"I guess it's like padding the score with extra runs to protect your lead in the game," Rich said.

"You could look at it that way," Tom said. "I tend to think of it as having an extra pitcher in your starting rotation. A lot of teams have five, but if you have six solid starters, then you're in much better shape if one of them gets hurt."

In Tom's case, the injured pitcher was the stock market crash of 2008 and 2009. The Pepperdino brothers had a knack for retiring at market peaks. Within a year and a half of Tom's retirement, the market bottomed out in March 2009. From the peak of the market in October 2007 through the trough in March 2009, the S&P 500 dropped 58 percent, while small caps fell 59 percent and international holdings declined 62 percent (see Exhibits 9.1 and 9.2). Tom looked around at his community of retired friends. Many had seen their cash flow dry up because they had everything invested in the stock market or real estate.

"I was worried, of course," Tom said. "But I wasn't overly concerned because I knew I had over two years of cash flow before I needed to rely on earnings from my portfolio."

Tom and his wife did cut back on their spending during 2008 and 2009. They made several baseball trips around the U.S., but they didn't go to Europe as they had planned to do. They ended up spending about $150,000 in 2009, down from their initial budget of $180,000.

The following year, 2010, the stock market grew and their financial advisor started pointing out some healthy gains in their small caps. That's when they revisited their cash flow ladder to prepare for the years beyond their original four-year plan. They harvested some gains from their small-cap assets and put them toward their cash flow savings for year five, along with the $30,000 they had saved in 2009. Three years into their cash flow ladder, they were pretty much set for year five. Since then, they had been making similar preparations for year six.

"That makes a lot of sense," Rich said. He liked the stability of the cash flow ladder.

"The cash flow ladder sure helped me sleep better at night, knowing our basic income needs were met while the world seemed to be crashing all around us," Tom added. "I saw how bad it was for my brother originally and later many of my friends who didn't have this arrangement. Don't get me wrong; the cash flow ladder doesn't

Periods of Consecutive Negative Stock Returns for Dow Jones Industrial Average, 1928 to 2011

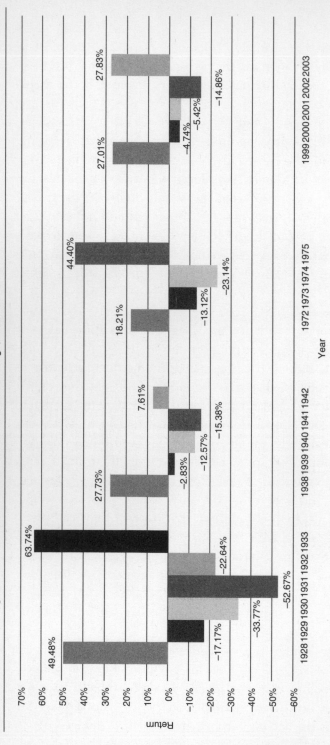

Source: Bloomberg and Dow Jones Industrial Average

Exhibit 9.1 Historically, there have been only a few times when the stock market has been negative for two or more consecutive years. Since the Great Depression, only once did the stock market experience negative returns for four consecutive years. There were two periods when the market was down for three consecutive years, with one of the three years being almost flat. In one period, the market was down for two consecutive years.

After each of these ugly periods, the following year was marked by a significant upturn in the market, but initially not enough to make up for the pullback of the prior years combined. This is why many investors are comfortable with a three- to five-year cash flow ladder. The thought is that three to five years of cash flow will allow them enough time to wait through the bad times before the market potentially recovers. This exhibit shows the Dow Jones Industrial Average data.

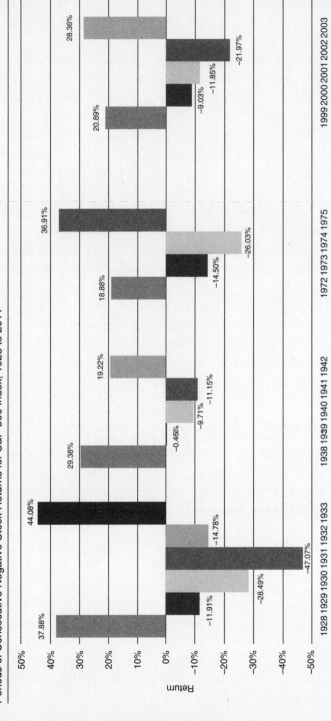

Periods of Consecutive Negative Stock Returns for S&F 500 Index, 1928 to 2011

Source: Bloomberg and Standard & Poor's
Data before 1957 are based on S&P 500 predecessor indices.

Exhibit 9.2 This exhibit shows the S&P 500 data and the data of its predecessor indices, in reference to the description given in Exhibit 9.1.

121

insulate you from losses, but it does give you time to wait out the ugly market until things get a little better."

The public address system interrupted Rich and Tom's conversation. It was United, announcing that the Vivas' flight to Houston was about to begin boarding. Rich bid adieu to Tom, thanking him for the advice.

"I hope you have a good trip to Los Angeles," Rich said. "We recommend the wine country if you get a chance to make it up there."

"That would be great," Tom said. "It's not going to happen on this particular trip, but I'm due for another visit to AT&T Park in San Francisco before long. Best of luck with your retirement. I think you'll find it to be a wonderful experience."

The Vivas returned to their gate and boarded the plane for Houston. After they buckled into their seats, Rich brought up the idea of the cash flow ladder to Peg.

"I think this could really help my peace of mind," Rich said. "I like the idea of having an annual budget. I like the idea that we'd be secured to some extent against market volatility. I like the idea of replenishing the cash flow ladder as we're able to do so."

Peg agreed.

"Let's see how this might work out," she said as she pulled out a pen and paper to make a note.

At a 4-percent withdrawal rate, they could afford to spend up to $640,000 a year based on their $16 million nest egg. However, when they discussed their goals, they had already agreed to an annual cash flow of about $300,000.

"I still feel good about $300,000," Rich said. "I have a hard time imagining we'll spend that much anyway."

Peg did the math. For a four-year cash flow ladder, they'd need to set aside $1.2 million.

"That's a lot of money," Rich said, "but it makes me feel better. I know we're supposed to be proactive with our money, but I don't mind putting some under the mattress. My mother would be proud."

"I totally agree," Peg said. "And if we don't spend $300,000 in any given year, we can reinvest the leftover funds or we can set them aside for future years on the ladder."

"Sounds like a plan," Rich said.

Rich thought about their return to Houston and his relatively open-ended schedule.

"I enjoyed chatting with Tom," Rich said. "His example is inspiring to me when it comes to the idea of finding something I can do while in retirement. I have no desire to tour around visiting sports stadiums, but I wouldn't mind coming up with a plan for the two of us to visit as many wineries as possible."

"Do you remember Ann, who worked with Greg?" Peg responded. "She had a goal to run a marathon in every state of the union and she actually did it."

"Maybe for me it will simply be to do the things we haven't had time to do all these years," Rich replied.

Peg shook her head.

"That's too vague," she said. "Besides, we don't want to just travel all of the time. I think you need to find some sort of hobby that you can do at home in Houston. Remember how you used to talk about how much you loved sailing that one chance you had at summer camp as a teenager? Maybe you could get a sailboat, or maybe you could get more involved with other groups like the industry association you work with. That reminds me: I was thinking you should write a column for one of the trade publications. I bet they'd like to hear from someone with your experience."

"Maybe so," Rich answered. "Writing never really occurred to me, but that could be an interesting challenge. I'll tell you this much: I never thought I'd see the day when Peg Viva encouraged me to get a sailboat."

Peg laughed.

"Knowing you, I have no doubt you will come up with the perfect thing that suits you, Rich. I just hope it doesn't become an obsession!"

Chapter 10

Trusted Advisor

Rich walked into Olivette, the restaurant at the Houstonian Hotel, Club & Spa, and spotted his pastor, Reverend Jim Conroy, reading the newspaper at a table near the corner window. The two men had a standing breakfast meeting that they'd maintained over the previous six years, about the time Pastor Conroy started at Houston's Grace Methodist Church. Jim was one of those men who would be successful at anything he put his mind to. Rich had wondered before just how wealthy Jim would be had his interest been in worldly pursuits, rather than spiritual.

Jim was in his early 60s and had wisdom beyond his years. He was the most perceptive person Rich had ever known, which came in quite handy in Jim's line of work. Somehow, Jim could laser in on the real issue regardless of what his parishioner or anyone else he was conversing with was willing to share. Yes, Jim would have been a very good businessman indeed, and Rich appreciated Jim's insight.

They met at the Houstonian, an exclusive social club near the church, every other month. The Houstonian is situated on acres of manicured lawns with beautiful towering trees. It may be best known as the address that the country's forty-first president, George H.W. Bush, used as his legal residence in Texas while occupying the White House. Bush still visited every once in a while, as did other Houston dignitaries like former secretary of state Jim Baker.

Richard looked forward to the meetings as a therapeutic opportunity to discuss his thoughts and worries one-on-one with Jim. Jim liked Rich's friendship, and appreciated his business savvy and advice on church money matters.

The two had missed a few of their breakfasts over the winter and spring, so this was their first meeting since the business sale. Pastor Conroy was interested to hear more about the sale and Rich's new life in retirement.

Rich filled him in on the details of the deal, his recent travel, and his plans for more travel.

"That sounds like some well-deserved rest and relaxation," Jim said, but he sensed that Rich was uneasy with the change. "How comfortable are you with this new chapter of your life?"

Pastor Conroy had long believed that virtually everyone can find the answers to many of life's problems and issues if they, or someone else, pose the right questions.

Rich nodded. "As you can imagine, I'm used to working. I don't know how I could just flip that switch off. Fortunately I'm not bored."

Rich's experience was similar to other recent retirees who find their days flying by with activities, to the point they questioned how they had time to fit work in before retirement. For Rich, retirement had been focused on finances, his life's journey, and travel—mostly in that order.

"Peg and I have been on several trips, which has been great because work used to always interfere with vacation time," Rich said. "I also spend a fair amount of time trying to figure out my financial future.

"I know I shouldn't complain. I sold the company for more money than I thought I would see in a lifetime, but it still concerns me that I'm no longer getting paid on a regular basis. So now I'm trying to figure out all the financial stuff that comes with retiring and not having regular income any longer."

Jim listened and gave Rich a reassuring smile.

"I know you make good decisions, Rich," he said. "If you didn't, you wouldn't have made it as far as you have in this world. I believe one day, when you look back, you'll have reason to be as proud of your success after retirement as you now feel about your career. Naturally, the next chapter of life comes with many unknowns. It's what's up ahead that is most concerning to you, Rich?"

It was a relief for Rich to share his true worries with someone he admired and respected.

"My desire to get it right is almost overwhelming," he replied. "Lately, I find myself obsessed about having a plan. My entire career I've known the path I wanted to take. But now I look out at my future and I feel a bit lost."

Rich had worked hard to build the life he had. He felt fortunate to have an incredible wife, and two loving and smart kids.

He continued, "I'm young enough to do just about anything I want. All those years of working long hours created a lot of pent-up demand for all those things I didn't have time for when I was too busy."

Rich was looking forward to enjoying his retirement without lots of worry. He wanted to be a good steward of the assets he had.

"In a nutshell, I just don't want to do anything stupid. I know that's not much of a financial plan—to not do something stupid. Greg would be real proud of that one!" Rich said.

Greg Webber had been Rich's first and only financial advisor until he died seven months before from a massive heart attack. Greg was also a member of Grace Methodist—Rich and Greg met there in the 1980s—and had been active in church business with Pastor Conroy.

"Greg would be proud of the way you're looking at this in a methodical and logical way, so don't beat yourself up too much," Jim said.

"I wish Greg was still around to help me out with all of this."

After Greg's death, his investment firm had attempted to spread his clients among its other advisors. The firm had matched Rich with a relatively young advisor named Brian Washington. They had only met once, and that was when Washington had discussed his thoughts for developing Rich's post-retirement investment plan. Rich thought

Washington had some good points, but there wasn't the level of confidence he felt with Greg.

"It's important to have advice that you trust," Pastor Conroy said. "And that includes financial matters. Think about it: You trust your doctor when it comes to health issues. I like to think you trust me when it comes to spiritual issues. It makes sense that you should have a trusted advisor when it comes to finances."

Jim pointed out that he relied on the church's business council, which included Rich, when it came to many of the church's business matters.

"But I also seek advice on all kinds of matters from the most trusted source available," he said.

"God?" Rich asked.

"Well, yes, I certainly pray for guidance on a daily basis. But I was actually talking about the Bible. You can find all sorts of practical advice in the Bible, especially the Book of Proverbs. To me, it's hard to find any better advice than the lessons in Proverbs."

Rich was somewhat familiar with the Old Testament Book of Proverbs, largely because of Pastor Conroy's sermons over the years. Some theologians credit King Solomon, a king of Israel and son of King David, with writing the book to share advice with his son. Others contend that various authors wrote the book and that King Solomon collected the stories and put them together for use as a training manual of sorts for those entering his service.

Either way, Rich was receptive to getting advice written or influenced by King Solomon. Solomon was believed to be the wisest man of his time. Not only that, he held a position in his society that would be equivalent to the wealthiest man in the world, the chief justice of the Supreme Court, the president of the United States, and the chairman of the Joint Chiefs of Staff—all rolled into one person.

Reverend Conroy had spent nearly a lifetime studying the Book of Proverbs. Rich was eager to learn more about his interpretation of such a revered text, especially one known for imparting wisdom and financial advice.

Pastor Conroy pulled out his well-worn Bible and flipped to Proverbs. He skimmed through a few pages while taking a sip of his coffee. He read several Proverbs with good advice related to investment and financial planning.

"Proverbs 10:31 and 15:7 teach that it takes a good person to give good advice. There are many people who can offer good quality advice," Jim said. "But if you're able to choose, it makes sense to me that you would take the advice from a good and decent person such as yourself, Rich. Someone with similar values."

That made sense to Rich. He thought about how he had inherently trusted Greg, partly because they were friends with similar interests and values.

"Proverbs 15:23 tells us that good advice is a joy to give," Jim continued. "I've found that to be true over the years. When I'm helping someone and I believe I've given the best advice I'm able to offer, I get a real sense of purpose and satisfaction. Hopefully the person you work with will enjoy sharing some of this wisdom and will do so in such a way that you'll enjoy working together.

"You know, Rich, after all those years of working tirelessly, life is too short to work with people who don't bring you a bit of joy," Jim added. "I suspect that if your new financial advisor delivers good advice, then your financial advisor will be a happy person."

Rich could relate to that. At ACS, he had felt good when he delivered the best possible products and services to his customers. It made sense to him that a good financial advisor would also get joy from delivering quality service and advice to him.

"Proverbs 18:13 and 18:15 stress the importance of being a good listener," Jim continued. "One of the most important attributes of an investment advisor should be the ability to communicate, and communication is based upon listening."

A financial advisor needs to fully understand an investor's goals to be capable of delivering good advice. With an understanding of the investor's goals, the advisor can then develop an appropriate plan and present it to the investor. Good communication keeps the dialogue open between the two and allows for better decision-making, especially during times when the path forward isn't clear.

Jim continued with his list of Proverbs that seemed to fit the bill.

"Rich, you probably want to work with someone who is also successful," he said. "Proverbs 10:4 reads that lazy men become poor while the hard-working get rich. And 14:23 states that work brings profits while pure talk brings poverty. In 22:29, the lesson is that hard work equates to success.

"Now, Rich, you and I both know hard-working people who aren't rich, especially those of us who choose to define wealth using different measures. So I'm not suggesting that all hard-working people are rich. I believe the author of Proverbs is indicating that those who work hard are more likely to do a better job, and therefore are more likely to create their own success.

"Likewise, hopefully those working hard are gaining wisdom," Jim said. "Wouldn't you feel more comfortable working with other successful and wise people who have done well for themselves?"

"I'm in complete agreement, Jim," Rich said. "I've always felt more comfortable dealing with hard-working, successful people. In fact, I completely agree with the general idea that the harder one works toward attaining their goals, the happier they will be whether they make the goals or not. The attitude seems to be more than half the battle."

Jim sat back and scanned the room of breakfast diners. He saw a large table of older men who appeared to be a regular breakfast group. They read their newspapers and occasionally stopped to sip coffee and chat.

"This isn't related to Proverbs, but I would think confidentiality is also an important issue," Jim said. "I assume most advisors are discreet and confidential when it comes to your money. I would be the first to leave if a financial advisor violated the trust of confidentiality."

Rich agreed. "Yes, loose lips have no place in this," he said. "I felt the same way at ACS."

"Here's another relevant Proverb," Jim added. "Don't do business with people you don't know. That's pretty straightforward. I would read that as a suggestion to get to know your financial advisor before you start doing business with him."

Rich liked the idea. "Yeah, it makes sense to get to know this new guy before I hire him to replace Greg. I really wish Greg was around to help me through this transition, but he's not. I thought the new guy made some good points in our first meeting, but I guess I just don't feel like I know him very well. I probably haven't given him a fair chance yet, because I haven't taken the time to get to know him."

Getting to know a financial advisor requires learning about the advisor's approach to investing and the way he or she works. Investors need to trust their advisor and be comfortable with the advisor's approach. Investors should look at an advisor's education, training designations, and experience. In most cases, investors are better off with someone who's been in the field for a while, rather than a rookie. Checking the website of the Financial Industry Regulatory Authority (FINRA) to see if other investors have filed complaints against an advisor is a good idea. Bear in mind that FINRA does not verify complaints, so it's possible to find illegitimate complaints posted on the site.

It's also important to do a little research on your potential advisor's firm. Many financial firms experienced less-than-flattering news during the recession and market collapse. A firm with a history of stability is desired. The firm is your safety net in case something goes wrong with your advisor. If your advisor dies or quits suddenly, a strong firm will help keep its investors on track. If an investor selects an incompetent advisor or a crook, a firm with deep pockets will be in a position to potentially help correct that situation. That doesn't mean the firm would make up for investment losses, but it would be in a position to reimburse an unlucky investor who was swindled.

"What's the best way to summarize all this advice?" Jim asked in a rhetorical manner. "I think it would be like this: You want to work with someone who is hard-working, who you believe to be a good and wise person, who enjoys giving advice, who is successful, and who is confidential about you and your portfolio.

"Although this isn't found in the book of Proverbs, another scripture that comes to mind is the golden rule," Jim added. "Do unto others as you would have them do unto you. In other words, find someone you believe will look out for your best interest with all your financial needs."

"That's how it was with Greg," Rich said. "I really trusted him, which was great. In hindsight, I may have been a little too hands-off with my investments because I knew Greg was handling them. Now I feel like I'm learning about investing from scratch."

With Greg as their financial advisor, Rich and Peg had placed all their investment funds in his trust. In recent months, Rich had considered the idea of spreading their newfound wealth between different investment companies, just for the sake of diversification. Both Ernie and Peg had advised against that approach. For one, investment advisors are likely to pay more attention to clients that place larger sums under their management. This made it even more important to select a trusted advisor in a reputable firm.

The importance of choosing the correct firm can be seen in the different experiences of investors at firms that have failed in recent years. Lehman Brothers and Bear Stearns were both respected firms with traditions of success, but both failed under extreme circumstances. In general, their investors' holdings were moved from the failed institutions to another firm, and the investors' portfolios were made whole—as long as they did not have holdings directly backed by the failed institutions. In the case of Bear Stearns, even some holdings backed by Bear were then backed by the acquiring firm of JP Morgan, though this is not always the case.

Investors with Bernie Madoff and Stanford Financial were less fortunate. In these cases, many of the firms' investments were fraudulent. For the most part, the investors were left empty-handed when the schemes failed.

An example of the value of depositing assets with a reputable investment firm can be illustrated by parking one's car in the garage of a neighbor's home. Of course, the difference is that cars depreciate over time, whereas the goal of the portfolio is to do the opposite. If the neighbor were to lose the home to foreclosure, the car owner would still have title and ownership of the car. The car owner would simply need to find a way to open the garage door.

Finding a trusted financial advisor is not to be taken lightly, as investors at Stanford or Madoff's investment firm would wholeheartedly agree. The old adage "too good to be true" comes to mind when evaluating advisors and investments. If investors in these firms had done their due diligence and asked the right questions, perhaps they would still have much of their portfolio and net worth.

Jim was still flipping through the Book of Proverbs to look for financial lessons. He had become intrigued with the search, similar to when he prepared for his sermons at Grace Methodist.

"Correct planning is mentioned in various verses in Proverbs including 15:22, 16:9, 19:21, and 20:18," he said, making a note on the small notebook he carried with him. "Finding the right advisor will help you plan correctly."

"That's what I'm attempting to accomplish," Rich replied.

"Ultimately, Proverbs 12:5, 12:15, 13:10, and 19:20 all convey that wisdom is the ultimate benefit of good advice," Jim added. "In fact, 12:15 reads that only a fool believes he needs no advice. Rich, the fact that you are even looking for guidance and advice is putting you in the right direction.

"As you can see, there's a great deal of practical advice in the Book of Proverbs," Jim continued. "But as your pastor, I would be remiss not to say that I believe the overwhelming message in Proverbs is that the ultimate goal in one's life is to seek wisdom and that God is still in control of the outcome. God wants us to be good stewards of what we have, so I commend you for seeking out someone who will help you with your plan."

As breakfast concluded, Rich picked up the bill and thanked Jim for the advice he needed to hear. Rich couldn't help but think that, if only someone like Pastor Conroy was in the investment business, he'd be ready to sign the dotted line right then.

Chapter 11

News versus Noise

It was a beautiful May Sunday in Houston: a balmy 85 degrees, blue skies, and a light breeze. Houstonians knew to make the most of these relatively pleasant days before the heat of summer descended on the city. Laura had joined Rich and Peg for the morning church service, and then the three went to lunch and dined al fresco at their favorite Mexican food restaurant, Escalante's. They filled up on chips and salsa, tacos, and enchiladas and lumbered back to the car for a restful afternoon. Rich and Peg dropped Laura off at her car at the church parking lot and headed for home.

"After a lunch like that I'm ready for a little siesta! I might just have to curl up for a nap," Peg said. "I feel like this day was made for relaxing."

"That would be great, but I'm afraid I won't be able to join you," Rich said. "Fred invited me over to watch the Astros game, and it starts in about an hour."

"Oh, I'd forgotten about that," Peg said. "I'm not sorry to miss that. Fred and relaxation don't exactly go hand-in-hand."

"Isn't that the truth," Rich said, shaking his head. "He isn't that bad, though, and I don't have so many friends that I can afford to go around turning down invitations. Besides, I haven't seen him in months. I really sort of feel sorry for the guy."

"Get ready. I bet Fred's going to grill you about your retirement and financial planning," Peg said.

"I know he will," Rich replied. "Maybe he'll help me figure out what not to do."

Peg laughed and nodded her head. "You may need a drink or two to put up with Fred for an entire afternoon. Just don't hesitate to call me if you get too drunk to drive home."

"Oh gosh, could you imagine?" Rich said. "I vow to not let Fred's worrisome ways get to me that much. Besides, I could just walk the five blocks back home, if it gets that bad."

Fred Burdon had retired from a sales career at Siemens five years earlier, at the age of 65. Rich and Fred worked on a project together back in the 1980s, and had ended up becoming friends. They seemed to have a lot in common, and they both lived in the same neighborhood. Fred did quite well for himself selling power plant components to utility companies in North America and South America, rising through the ranks and becoming a top sales executive for the company's North American division before he retired.

Fred was a charismatic guy, which made him a good salesman. Rich liked Fred's conversation, especially his wild stories about sales trips to places like Brazil and Argentina. But Rich hadn't seen as much of Fred in recent years. That was largely because Fred had grown increasingly anxious and difficult to be around since he left Siemens.

Fred had relished the thought of retirement—the concept of laying low and taking it easy. As it turned out, however, retirement had not been very good for Fred. He was a high-strung fellow. Before retirement, he channeled his stress and energy into getting the job done, but after he retired, he found himself with little to do except worry about his investment portfolio. Peg often remarked that Fred was one of those retirees who had failed to find a fulfilling diversion to make the most of his newfound freedom, and he therefore lacked meaning in his life.

Fred has been single since getting divorced about 10 years before. The divorce was very hard on Fred, partly because he didn't see it coming. It shouldn't have been that big of a surprise. His wife, Emily, had gotten worn down by Fred's anxiety. In the couple of years leading up to the divorce, Emily would go on weeks-long trips to stay with her sister in Arizona or to visit their adult son in Atlanta. It was evident to almost anyone paying attention that Emily was escaping Fred. Initially, Fred welcomed the alone time, but that changed when Emily returned from one of her trips to announce that she was filing for divorce and moving to Arizona.

Fred moped around for about a year before adjusting to his new life as a bachelor. He worked a lot and traveled to Atlanta from time to time to visit his son's family, including a couple of grandchildren. He went on fishing trips with the men's group at his church. After retirement, such diversions filled only a small fraction of Fred's free time.

For the most part, Fred dedicated his time and energy to his investment portfolio. He read the *Wall Street Journal* every morning and spent hours a day following economic and stock market news on the Internet and cable TV. Fred's obsession with economic news had not been good for his demeanor, and probably not good for his portfolio. More than once, Rich had seen Fred get up from lunch or a game to check his stocks and then call his financial advisor in a panic.

Rich felt a nagging sense of dread about this particular visit with Fred, his first since the business sale. He fully expected Fred to jump on the topic of retirement and personal finances. Rich was still charting his portfolio. As he had told Peg earlier, he was certain that Fred's approach was not a good example. Rich also felt a bit hypocritical, considering his recent obsession with his financial future and how his plan could impact his own success, or failure.

Fred was a big baseball fan, having played the game in high school and college. Like most Houstonians, Fred had followed the Astros all his life, even when they were originally established as the Colt .45s in 1962. He attended several games a year, and was among the critics who were bitter about Major League Baseball's decision to move the team from the National League to the American League. "Fifty years of history just uprooted like it didn't mean anything," Fred had said more than once.

Rich arrived for the game with a bag of chips and some salsa he'd picked up at Escalante's. Fred welcomed Rich in and poured him a glass of Malbec from a bottle he'd acquired in Argentina years before. Rich was pleased to find that Fred had also invited his neighbor and their mutual friend Tim Ida to watch the game with them. Fred fixed a sizable Dewar's on the rocks for himself as they sat down to watch the game on his flat-screen TV.

Tim Ida was a jack of all trades and entrepreneur extraordinaire. He had started all kind of businesses, from car washes to restaurants and real estate management companies. Tim was financially successful, but his net worth would probably have been higher if he had stuck with one or two of his many business concepts. He just never seemed to have enough hours in a day to manage all of his ventures. At 65, he still seemed to have boundless energy. He was one of those people who was constantly on the move. There would be no sitting back and taking it easy for Tim—even in retirement.

Before the umpire declared, "Play ball," Fred broached the subject of Rich's financial situation.

"Did the *Houston Business Journal* get it right—the details on the ACS sale?" Fred asked.

"Yes, it was pretty comprehensive," Rich said. "I talked with the reporter about it for a few minutes and laid out most of the details. I figured there weren't going to be too many secrets since the buyer was a public company. Still, it's always strange to read about yourself in the newspaper, especially at that level of detail."

"A few of my businesses made the newspaper over the years," Tim said. "Most of my deals were smaller than yours, so the press didn't seem overly interested in the financials, fortunately."

"Well, having a lot of money to worry about is a good thing, I suppose," Fred said. "You used to work with Greg Webber, before he passed away, didn't you? Have you found another financial advisor to help you out, or are you going to tackle it yourself?"

"I wish Greg was still around to help me out. I met with another guy at Greg's firm a few months ago to get the ball rolling," Rich said. "He seemed to know what he was talking about. He outlined a strategy for me to think about. We're supposed to meet again next month to hammer out more details. I probably should have already settled this by now, but I've been taking my time and sort of putting it off."

"I do most of my trading online," Tim said. "Sure, I enjoy getting the viewpoints of a professional from time to time, but most of them want to stick with long-term planning. I like to keep my money in motion."

"I would refer you to my guy, but I don't know if he'd accept any of my referrals," Fred said to Rich. "He tolerates me, but I don't think he's all that happy to hear from me."

Rich thought it would be polite to act like he didn't understand, even though he did.

"What do you mean?" he asked.

Fred went on. Because of his intense interest in his portfolio, he was always calling his broker to tinker with his investments, asset allocation, and the like. Fred had his own ideas about how to interpret economic indicators, and he didn't want to let anything slip by him. His advisor, on the other hand, encouraged Fred to relax and take a long-term approach based on logic and fundamentals. He discouraged Fred's tendency to react emotionally to the latest headlines.

"That's hard for me," Fred acknowledged. "Ever since I retired, I've been worried that I have only a certain amount of money to work with, both for my future and my grandkids' futures. I don't want to be asleep at the switch."

"I can definitely relate to that," Rich said. "That has been one of the hardest parts of this transition for me. I don't feel comfortable spending money when I'm not earning it anymore."

"Exactly," Fred answered. "So I try to make sure I'm staying on top of everything. I want to know how the markets are trending. I want to know how different companies are performing. I want to be completely informed."

"I can understand that, but if that's the case, why do you even have a financial advisor?" Rich asked.

"Well, for one, I realize I'm not a professional. I have my opinions, but they're not always correct," Fred said. "There's also the reality that I need someone to temper my anxiety. Besides, I like to have someone to bounce my ideas off of from time to time, and occasionally he brings something of interest to me."

"So there's tension with your financial advisor because you're too involved? That sounds to me like maybe you should work with someone else, someone who doesn't mind that you want to be involved," Tim said.

Fred smiled and shrugged. "I can see why you'd say that, but to be totally honest, I also realize my own limits when it comes to investing. I've made plenty of mistakes, particularly a few years ago. My advisor helps keep me steady. I feel like I'm addicted to information, but all these tidbits of news tend to make me panic. My advisor offers useful perspective. He also tells me I should turn off the news."

Rich marveled at Fred's introspection. He had picked up on Fred's anxiety many times, but he didn't realize that Fred was self-aware about it. Fred's realization of his own shortcomings caused Rich to feel pity for his friend, rather than annoyance.

"I've been accused of being overly active with my portfolio," Tim said. "I'm not like Fred where I'm trying to constantly predict every market move. I simply like to stay active. I feel like I need to be selling or buying almost daily. In fact, sometimes I buy in the morning and sell in the afternoon."

"Why would you do that?" Rich asked. "How do you have time for it?"

Tim shrugged. "Well, retirement has given me plenty of time. I like to keep my portfolio active because I figure that's better than just letting it sit there."

"I'm trying to go the opposite direction," Fred said. "I'm trying to do a better job of following my financial advisor's advice now. He preaches this concept called 'news versus noise.'"

News is the substantive information that affects investments, such as corporate earnings and other hard data. Noise is the frenzy surrounding economic news—the type of frenzy that sometimes prompts kneejerk reactions among investors. In the days of 24-hour media dedicated to covering every market development, every political speech, and every controversy, it's easy for investors to get carried away with the noise.

The challenge for investors is to tune out the noise and concentrate on substantive news that contributes to making informed long-term decisions. While information is more prevalent than ever before, qualified interpretation of the information is often lacking. Too often, investors take short-term information that doesn't have long-term implications and use it as the basis for investment decisions that have long-term ramifications (see Exhibit 11.1).

For instance, during a volatile market, some investors may make the mistake of setting arbitrary benchmarks for getting out of the market. An investor might say, "If the market drops another 2 percent, I'm selling out," or "If my portfolio drops to $1 million, I'm selling everything." This seems particularly irrational in a volatile period, when markets can move more than 2 percent in a day. Although it's understandable to cut your losses, doing so based upon an arbitrary number or percentage decline rarely serves the investor well over the long term.

"I'm the kind of guy who will question the validity of my investment plan if it looks like the market is going to be down," Fred said. "I don't want to take one step forward and then two steps back, or even two steps forward and one step back.

"That's what I butt heads with my advisor about," Fred continued. "I understand that decisions should be based on fundamentals, but I don't think it's good to ignore the latest news. I'm just looking for a leg up, a little advantage. My broker wants to focus on the overall plan and whether it's achieving my objectives and goals over time.

"In fact, although I still refer to him as a broker from time to time, his actual title is financial advisor. Buying and selling stocks is just a small part of his overall business. He puts a lot of emphasis on financial planning, and he works with me to maintain a portfolio that works toward reaching my goals and objectives," Fred said.

"I can't take that type of plodding approach," Tim said. "My goal is to be proactive. No waiting around on the market for me. I'll make something happen regardless of what is taking place in the overall economy or markets."

The approach of Fred's financial advisor sounded rational, Rich thought, but he understood Fred's motivation to stay involved and

Investor Returns: not the same as *Investment* Returns

What caused the difference?

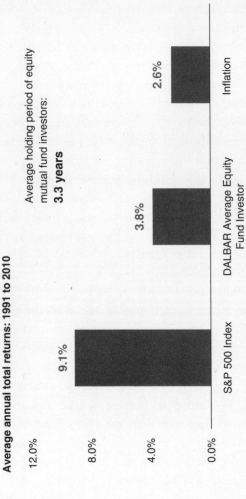

Average annual total returns: 1991 to 2010

Average holding period of equity mutual fund investors:

3.3 years

S&P 500 Index	9.1%
DALBAR Average Equity Fund Investor	3.8%
Inflation	2.6%

12.0%
8.0%
4.0%
0.0%

Source: "Quantitative Analysis of Investor Behavior, 2011," DALBAR, Inc.; used with permission. For illustrative purposes only. Past performance does not guarantee future results. The S&P 500 is an unmanaged, weighted index comprising 500 widely held common stocks varying in composition and is unavailable for direct investment. Average Equity Fund Investor is comprised of the cash flow of 4,585 equity funds as classified by ICI (Investment Company Institute). The returns is represented by the change in total equity mutual fund assets after excluding sales, redemptions and exchanges. This method of calculation captures realized and unrealized capital gains, dividends, interest, trading costs, sales charges, fees, expenses, and any other costs. After calculating investor returns in dollar terms, two percentages are calculated for the period examined. Performance calculated assumes reinvestment of all dividends and capital gains. Total return rate is determined by calculating the investor return dollars as a percentage of the net of the sales, redemptions, and exchanges for the period. Holding period reflects the length of time the average investor holds a fund if the current redemption rate persists. It is the time required to fully redeem the account. Retention rates are expressed in years and fractions of years. Over the time period 1991–2010, the average equity fund investor held their mutual funds for an average of 3.3 years.

Exhibit 11.1 Investors often miss out on returns when they are too quick to shift strategies and jump from one investment to another. Many confuse activity with productivity. Investors with a top-quality strategy are likely to outperform those constantly searching for higher returns.

make the most of his assets. Tim's approach didn't make much sense to Rich. He felt as if Tim was changing investments like he changed chairs while watching the game. He must have been up and down over a dozen times in the first two innings alone.

"What changed, Fred?" Richard asked. "You said you've been trying to heed your financial advisor's advice."

Fred shook his head as he took a sip of scotch. He grabbed his BlackBerry to glance at it, but then set it down in an apparent show of self-restraint. He found it easier to do this on Saturdays and Sundays, when the markets were closed.

"The stock market crash," Fred responded. "When things were going really bad and the market was tanking a few years ago, I was freaking out and calling my advisor all the time. I wanted to cash out, and he was telling me, 'No, you've got to ride this out.' It was obvious to me that we were getting wiped out, and so I went with my gut. I cashed out 80 percent of my portfolio and put the money in a savings account. That was March of 2009."

"What about the other 20 percent?" Richard asked.

"That's all my advisor could convince me to leave in the market," Fred responded. "He kept talking about how the market was trading at a very low P/E multiple, and that fundamentally, the stock market was inexpensive. I was afraid I was about to lose everything—my entire life savings—and I panicked. My net worth was down considerably, but I figured I could afford to lose the 20 percent left in the market. So I left it in."

"But that's what changed," Fred continued. "My remaining investments in the market have doubled since I cashed out. I lost millions on the rest of my portfolio by selling it all when it was almost worthless. I've reinvested since then, but there's no question that I definitely made a mistake."

Panic selling has a compounding effect. Investors sell when the value of their holdings is down, and then lose the chance to ride back up once the market takes a turn for the better. Investors who sell at a bottom often only feel comfortable reinvesting once the market surpasses the prior high. Although most people say they want to buy low and sell high, it is easier to sell low and buy high. When the market is high, usually things are positive and investors are optimistic.

When the market is low, things are negative and it feels more comfortable being out of the market. That's actually the time to add to your holdings—when the market is down (see Exhibit 11.2).

"Wow. That's something," Richard said. "So in your broker's language, you succumbed to the 'noise' and lost sight of the 'news.'"

Fred nodded. "It's not like I'm a different person these days. I still stress about the market, and I still want to be active in managing my portfolio. But at least I'm trying to take a longer view—to look at things logically and pay attention to the fundamentals. I'd be in much better shape today if I had taken a longer view back in March 2009. It's still hard for me to control my reactions to the constant news and turn off the worry."

"Don't you mean the constant 'noise'?" Rich asked.

"Touché, Rich!" Fred acknowledged.

"Personally, I like all the noise," Tim said. "It works for me. I buy, sell, and buy again—sometimes the same holding all in one day. My CPA calls me a trader, not an investor. I can't recall the last time I had a long-term capital gain or loss—almost all of my trading is characterized as short-term when it comes to taxes."

The baseball game had reached the third inning. The Astros were up 7–0 over the lowly Chicago Cubs.

Fred stood up and gulped the remaining two fingers of scotch in his glass. He poured himself a refill and opened the laptop sitting on the coffee table. He logged on and scanned the headlines on Bloomberg and CNBC. The market had dropped 200 points on Friday because of political turmoil in the European Union. The talking heads were projecting more losses on Monday.

"I'm going to run and call my advisor's office and leave a message for him to call me back before tomorrow's open," Fred said. "I don't want my stocks to get killed tomorrow, and I've got a couple of ideas to soften the blow. You keep those Astros in line for me, okay?"

"No problem, I've got it covered," Rich said.

"Good idea, Fred," Tim said. "I'm getting up early tomorrow to see where I want to re-allocate some of my holdings."

Rich watched Fred scurry down the hall and couldn't help but feel sorry for him. He decided right then that he would not let the "noise" drown out a more rational investment approach based on

Investors navigating through equity markets can experience both ups and downs in the market on a year-by-year basis

1980 to 2011 calendar-year returns and market corrections (S&P 500 Index)

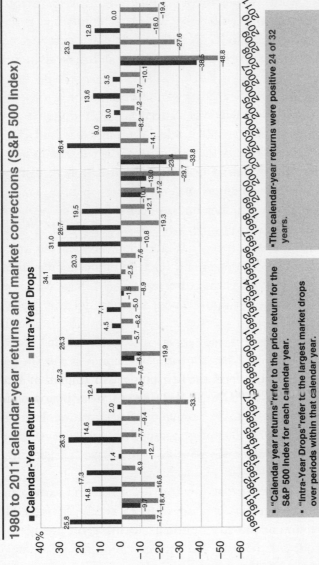

■ Calendar-Year Returns ■ Intra-Year Drops

■ "Calendar year returns" refer to the price return for the S&P 500 Index for each calendar year.

■ "Intra-Year Drops" refer to the largest market drops over periods within that calendar year.

■ The calendar-year returns were positive 24 of 32 years.

Past performance is no guarantee of future results. This chart is for illustrative purposes only. Source: Ned Davis Research, Inc., as of 12/31/11. Standard & Poor's market returns represented by the S&P 500 Index return and do not include dividends. Refer to the Index Definitions pages for listing of index definitions. Unlike mutual funds, indices are not managed and do not incur fees or expenses. It is not possible to invest directly in an index.

Exhibit 11.2 Although annually the market has closed higher 75 percent of the last 32 years, the average intra-year pullback from peak to trough is almost 15 percent. Unfortunately short-term volatility is simply par for the course. Those constantly attempting to get out before a pullback often end up missing the longer-term positive returns in the market.

logic and reason. Rich also made a mental note to avoid being around Fred during the hours when the exchanges were open for trading. Watching a baseball game with Fred when the equity markets were open would either make him laugh or cry; watching a game with both Fred and Tim when the markets were open would make him run for cover.

Blocking out the noise in favor of the news made good sense to Rich. For Fred, apparently, it was easier said than done. But Rich hadn't been watching all that much television news. He and Peg subscribed to the *Houston Chronicle*, and he read the news online nearly every day. Most of the financial news he paid attention to came from columnists and the daily business page in the newspaper.

Rich thought about whether he had been affected by news coverage when it came to his investment decisions. It occurred to him that the influence had been different. While Fred overreacted to news developments, often to his detriment, Rich found all of the information to be paralyzing. Rather than overreacting, Rich was inclined to sit on his hands because he didn't know what to do. But that could also be detrimental.

The economic recession and uncertain recovery didn't help. For several years, Rich had seen mostly bad economic news in the media. Why would he want to get involved with investing in that kind of environment? Rich took comfort in the idea of just stashing his money away in a bank account and not worrying about investing. But he also realized it was not a practical approach, especially considering his plans with Peg to grow their net worth, travel, and leave a legacy for the children.

Maybe Rich's reluctance to act on his portfolio wasn't all that different than Fred's kneejerk reactions? In each case, both would be better served by tuning out the noise and focusing on the news.

Fred returned, and he and Tim began discussing what the next day might bring, while Rich lost himself in his own thoughts for a few minutes. He realized that, although the three had much in common, their outlooks and approaches to investing were quite different.

For the first time, Rich understood that his fear of the unknown future was delaying his financial plan. He was in a state of paralysis by analysis, and apparently found comfort in doing nothing. Fred, on the other hand, was in a continual state of panic as he monitored every bit of economic data regardless of its significance. Tim was just bored. Although he seemed to have an investment strategy closer to Fred's than Rich's, Tim's motivation was a result of the need to be proactive regardless of being right or wrong. Tim could not differentiate between being proactive and productive. Tim traded simply to trade, just as a runner runs to run.

The trip to Fred's taught Rich more about investment psychology than he had ever imagined. He knew he didn't want to adopt either Fred's or Tim's investment strategy—and he also knew it was time to begin implementing a plan of his own.

Chapter 12

Family Dynamics

R ich started the Mercedes SUV and turned to Peg as they pulled out of the driveway.

"This ought to be interesting," he said softly, almost talking to himself.

Rich and Peg were both excited and a bit nervous. They were driving to Houston's George Bush Intercontinental Airport to pick up their son, Patrick, who was arriving home after a long flight from Paris.

"I wonder if we'll even recognize him," Peg said.

"Let's just hope for no major surprises," Rich responded.

Patrick had completed two years at Louisiana State University before deciding the previous summer to "take a break" from school and travel around Europe. His summer trip had stretched into the fall as he explored the continent, and he ended up staying in Paris for a few months. The Vivas weren't really sure what Patrick was doing with his time in Paris, and they had tried more than once to convince him to return home and get back to school.

Patrick was a gifted painter; it came naturally to him. He was drawn to Europe—its history and culture. His trip was an opportunity to see classic works of art and architecture and meet like-minded artists in magnificent cities like Prague, Venice, and Paris.

The Vivas were initially supportive of Patrick's trip. While it could be a hard ideal to practice, they had always felt their children's best path to a happy and successful life was through pursuit of their interests and passions. Rich and Peg had agreed to fund the majority of Patrick's trip. That was because Patrick had planned to return home after a summer of travel and return to school. He was planning to major in art at LSU.

Patrick's agenda had changed during his travels, however. Recently, he had been e-mailing his parents about the beauty of Paris and his desire to stay there and pursue a career in painting. He liked the bohemian scene in Paris: the sidewalk cafes, the myriad art galleries, and the seemingly thousands of young artists all pursuing their dreams. "This is where I was meant to be," Patrick told his parents on a phone call.

After taking a hard line against sending more money to Patrick when he extended his trip beyond the summer, Rich had relented to Peg's argument that they should occasionally send Patrick more cash. Peg had convinced Patrick to come home for the holidays partly by offering to send him money in the interim. The Vivas tried to accept the viewpoint that Patrick's extended European odyssey was his version of studying abroad.

Patrick had been reluctant to come home for the holidays because he wanted to experience Christmas in Paris. He held leverage in the argument because he could have just refused his parents' invitation for the holiday trip. To secure his cooperation, Peg had agreed to buy him a ticket to return to Paris. But she and Rich definitely intended to try to talk some sense into their son and convince him to stay, or at least make solid plans to return to school in the near future.

Rich was less than thrilled with Patrick's behavior. He was supportive of Patrick's pursuit of art, but he didn't like the way he seemed to be finagling money out of his mother. The example of Skip Troutman hovered in the back of Rich's mind. Skip's recent arrest in Los Angeles was just the latest instance of Ernie having to bail out his son.

It seemed to Rich that Skip had lost touch with reality somewhere along the way. His drug use was obviously a big part of the problem, but Rich thought Skip was hopelessly spoiled—to the point that he had no concept of earning his own way through life. Patrick had always been a good kid, but Rich thought the Paris escapade demonstrated tendencies frighteningly similar to Skip.

Still, Rich was excited and happy to see his son. The Vivas had never gone six months without seeing their son before.

"I think we've got to view this as an opportunity, rather than a problem," Rich said as they sat in traffic on the freeway. "It sounds trite, but that approach helped me in business from time to time."

"I like the optimism, but I'm not sure what you're talking about," Peg said. "You mean an opportunity to convince Pat to go back to school?"

"I guess I'm not sure, either," Rich answered. "I just think we'll get better results if we approach Pat positively. I think we could alienate him pretty quickly if we act like we've got a big problem on our hands. I wouldn't be surprised if he gets defensive about this."

They drove in silence for a couple of minutes. Rich focused on the possible opportunities at hand. The obvious opportunity was the chance to persuade Patrick to return to Baton Rouge and get his degree. Rich thought about his own life and the crossroads he faced with retirement. The "opportunity" that had consumed Rich was the development of a financial road map for the rest of his life. He had been preoccupied with the business sale and his own financial planning for months.

Would that be relevant to Patrick? At first blush, no, Rich thought. On the other hand, Patrick apparently wanted to pursue his interest in art. Most artists aren't known for their financial stability. So maybe financial planning would be particularly relevant to Patrick. If Patrick could learn to manage his money wisely, he would have more liberty to pursue his dream of being an artist. Also, investment acumen would help Patrick one day when he would likely inherit considerable net worth from his parents.

Rich didn't want to spoil his son's dream. But he did have a feeling that Patrick was probably going about it the wrong way. If Patrick was serious about being a professional artist, he would need to find a way to make the job financially sustainable, or else he would eventually be forced to quit and do something else. Patrick's apparent decision to drop out of school and become a starving artist in Paris might be romantic, but it was unlikely to help Patrick make a serious career as an artist over the long term.

Rich explained his line of thinking to Peg.

"It reminds me of my old high school friend Jimmy Lankerton," Peg said. "He played guitar in bar bands until he was about 30, always just scraping by. He finally went back to school and got a music degree. Now, he runs a guitar school down in Galveston. He still plays in bands—the last I heard, anyway—but he has the foundation of the guitar school to pay the bills."

"Exactly," Rich said. "Somewhere along the way, I heard that wisdom is learning from your mistakes, and true wisdom is learning from the mistakes of others without experiencing the mistake yourself. I can't say that I was very wise when I was 21, but I did listen to my parents, even when I didn't want to admit it. I wonder if we can make this point to Pat—not only the importance of school, but also the importance of financial planning?"

"Maybe," said Peg. "He's so young and idealistic. I wouldn't be surprised if he thought being a starving artist was actually good for him."

"Well, there's only so much we can do," Rich said. "And maybe all we can do now is plant the seeds of thinking about the idea of financial stability, saving money, and investing for the future."

"This is starting to sound familiar," Peg responded with a laugh.

"You know how I am," Rich said. "I tend to get caught up in things."

The Vivas discussed their plan as they walked into the international terminal. They were just in time for Patrick's arrival.

Patrick exited customs, walked into the terminal, and raced over to his parents to give them a big hug. Rich and Peg were thrilled to see him. The Parisian painter version of their son definitely looked different and older than the student who had departed for Europe six months earlier. Patrick had grown a full beard for the first time in his life. He'd shaved his head and was wearing a black beret—also firsts. Peg noticed that he looked a bit leaner.

"Welcome back, son," Rich said. "We've got a lot to talk about."

Patrick quickly settled back into his old bedroom and life around the Viva house. He loved the minimalist lifestyle of the traveler—sleeping in hostels, on couches, and even on the occasional park bench. But he was also grateful for the comforts of home and his own bed. He watched lots of TV over the first couple of days because it was refreshing to soak in familiar culture and watch programs in English. He cooked a couple meals for his parents, including a French fish soup called bouillabaisse, to demonstrate some of the exotic flavors he'd encountered during his travels.

The Vivas wanted to take Patrick out for dinner on Thursday evening. They first thought of going out for pizza or Mexican food, but decided that something more elegant was in order. They wanted to celebrate Patrick's return, even if it was only temporary. They also thought a nicer place might remind Patrick of the importance of having money and the finer things in life that accompany it. Lastly, they wanted a place that would lend itself to good conversation.

They deliberately chose Thursday night because they knew Laura had a game with her indoor soccer team, and Rich and Peg believed their conversation with Patrick would be best suited for just the three of them. Laura would be able to join them at another time, but this dinner was dedicated to Patrick's future. Rich hoped they could have a serious discussion.

Rich and Peg decided on Tony's, the same restaurant they had selected for Patrick's high school graduation dinner. The valets met the Vivas with a smile as they drove up to the front door of the fashionable establishment. You knew you were a really good customer when Nacho, the head valet, recognized you well enough to forego the typical claim check. Scott, the manager, welcomed the Vivas by name and had reserved a table off to the side apart from the other tables to provide more privacy, as Rich had requested.

As they ordered dinner, they thought their plan was working when Patrick mentioned that he hadn't eaten at a fancy restaurant since before he went overseas.

"Tony's reminds me a bit of the restaurant in Paris where I washed dishes to help make ends meet," Patrick remarked. "You can't believe how many dishes get dirty when people are eating multiple courses like this. It wasn't very much fun, but at least I was able to find a job."

"Your mom and I are proud that you found a job in Paris," Rich said. "In fact, I'm a bit envious that you are following your passion and making your own way.

"However, we want to run something by you. Your mother and I have some ideas about how you could make this art thing work long-term."

Patrick looked down and took a deep breath. "Okay. I figured this was coming. Let me just say that I think the 'art thing,' as you call it, is already working. Besides, you just said you're proud of me."

"We'll always be proud of you, Patrick," Rich replied. "But would your art sales and income from dishwashing be enough to live on without our help?"

Peg stepped in before Patrick had a chance to bristle up.

"We have nothing against you pursuing your passion for art in Paris," she said. "We just can't keep paying for it. We've covered you for a summer and the fall semester. I consider that to be like paying for a semester abroad. But that semester is over now and you've got to decide whether you really want to be an artist in Paris or come back home and go to school.

"There's nothing wrong with being an expatriate artist in Paris if you really want to go down that road," she continued. "But it's our opinion that you should finish your college degree first."

"I'm learning way more in Paris than I ever would at LSU," Patrick replied. "I'm meeting all sorts of great artists, and they're teaching me more than I ever learned in any college class. And I am making some money. I've sold a few paintings at street fairs, and my part-time job washing dishes at the café is helping to make ends meet."

"That is good," Rich said. "But you're still paying rent to sleep on a couch in an overcrowded house, right? I'm pretty sure you're going to get tired of that eventually. We want to help you, but we're not going to send money to you to continue the way you're going.

"Here's an idea we want you to consider. We have a proposal for you."

Rich proceeded to explain the plan that he and Peg had come up with. It was both a financial incentive to encourage Patrick to finish his degree and a lesson in financial planning.

If Patrick would agree to return to LSU and work toward completing his degree, his parents would start a joint investment portfolio for him. The Vivas would invest $10,000 in startup cash and then match each of Patrick's contributions on a two-to-one basis. Patrick would be required to actively monitor the portfolio and meet with a financial advisor twice a year.

After graduation, Patrick could begin drawing cash out of the portfolio, as long as he put the money toward his career.

"How could I spend money on my career?" Patrick said. "I thought you had a career to earn money, not to spend it."

"You're right about that in most cases," said Rich. "But if you pursue art, you're looking at a non-traditional career. We think you can be successful because you're so talented. But we also think you're fighting an uphill battle. We're trying to find a way to give you a better chance of success."

"There are so many talented painters who never make money as an artist," Peg added. "It takes more than talent. You need to have a plan and the means to pursue it. You could use the investment funds to lease studio space, open a gallery, buy supplies—stuff like that. Or you might decide you want to get a master's degree."

Patrick perked up for a moment. "A studio would be cool," he said.

The Vivas hoped the plan would achieve a few of their goals. First, they wanted to convince Patrick to finish his degree and drop his hair-brained scheme to move to Paris. Second, they hoped it would teach Patrick the value and reward of financial planning. This type of intervention could hopefully steer Patrick toward responsible decisions and away from the spoiled behavior of someone like Skip Troutman. Third, the plan could provide the financial infrastructure for Patrick to at least try to pursue his dream of being an artist, which by all accounts would not be an easy way to make money.

"Think about it: If you invested just $100 a month, you could have over $20,000 or more to put toward renting a studio when you graduate," Peg said.

"I don't know," Patrick said. "It's a really nice offer and I appreciate it. I like the idea of having some money to help me continue painting. But I don't think you have to be rich to be successful at painting. I think the best art in the world comes from pain and suffering. A lot of the masters painted their best work when they had no money. Think of Vincent Van Gogh and his beautiful work."

"Exactly, Van Gogh was so depressed that he cut his own ear off, and later killed himself," Rich replied.

"Patrick, we simply want you to be self-reliant and happy over the long term. What if Dad and I weren't here to help you?" Peg reasoned.

"We want you to have the best of both worlds—an opportunity to pursue your passion, and possibly your life calling, while still having a formal education, in case you decide to pursue other interests in the world of art in the future," Rich said.

"Just give it some thought," Rich said. "We want you to come back to the United States and finish your degree, and we're willing to support you to do that. When you finish your degree, then you'll have some startup money to get your career going, and you could even go back to Europe at that point."

"I'll think about it," Patrick said. "I'd also be willing to take that $10,000 up-front and spend it pursuing my art career in Paris now."

They all had a laugh at that, which helped break the tension of the conversation.

"Unlikely," Rich responded.

Later that night, as Peg and Rich were getting ready for bed, Peg brought up their dinner conversation with Patrick.

"Do you think Pat's going to agree to any of this?" she asked.

"It's hard to know," Rich said. "I hope it at least gets him thinking about it."

"One thing has occurred to me about all this," Peg said. "What about Laura? It wouldn't be fair for us to give this money to Patrick and not find a way to help her as well."

"That's true," Rich said. "But it doesn't seem like we need to hold her hand as much as Patrick needs it."

They discussed Laura's situation. The 25-year-old had a chemical engineering job at Exxon in Houston. She was making decent money and participated in the 401(k) program at work. Laura seemed to understand the value of saving money and planning for the future.

"She's still pretty young," Peg said. "Maybe we should start an investment portfolio for Laura and help contribute to it. Then we could also ask her to participate in managing it."

Rich liked the idea. They would offer to open an investment portfolio for Laura and contribute the equal amount of startup cash as they offered Pat, $10,000. From that point, they would match Laura's contributions dollar for dollar. In exchange, Laura would be expected to take an active role in monitoring the portfolio and meet with her financial advisor at least twice a year.

"We could present this to Laura as a retirement plan," Rich said. "I know she's contributing to her 401(k) plan at work, but we should ask if she's maxing out her contributions. If not, our gift would allow her to use part of this to subsidize her living expenses if she is unable to afford to max out her 401(k). If she is already maxing out, this would allow her to save more in a taxable account, which we would then match."

"I feel good about the idea of helping the kids out, but doing it with some structure," Peg said. "Maybe we'll all figure out this financial planning thing together."

Patrick and Laura had plans to meet that night for a drink at the City Centre. Rich and Peg dropped Patrick off at the bar, because Laura had offered to give him a ride home.

Patrick was sipping a glass of red wine when Laura showed up in her soccer sweats. She ordered a low-carb beer.

"Sorry I'm not more presentable," Laura said. "I ended up playing in two games tonight and ran out of time to get home for a shower. Besides, I can't stay out too long because tomorrow is regular workday for me. How was the dinner with Mom and Dad?"

"Not bad. It's hard to have a bad dinner at Tony's," he said. "As you can imagine, they want me to return to the States, and they're actually offering me money to come back."

"Money? I wish I had run off to explore the world to be lured back home with some money!" Laura laughed.

"Listen, Laura, I'm not just goofing around like you and Mom and Dad seem to think," Patrick said. "You know how doctors have a residency when they get out of school, or how attorneys clerk at different law firms between semesters before they graduate? I'm doing my own internship abroad and working hard at it."

"I don't think you're goofing around," Laura said. "But I think your point is a little off the mark. Doctors don't go into residency until they've been formally trained. Lawyers don't clerk until they've been to law school. I think Mom and Dad just want you to finish school before you explore your dreams as an artist.

"I know they seem annoying, but I really think they want what is best for you," Laura added. "It's not like college life is such a drag. Sometimes I wish I could go back."

"I had fun in Baton Rouge, without a doubt, but Paris is better," Patrick said. "I know Mom and Dad care about me and only want what's best for me, but I don't know what to do. What do you think?"

"First of all, I think it's great that you have traveled and have experienced the world," Laura said. "But I also think it's important to get a college degree. You never know where it could lead. There are a lot of talented people out there who would be a lot better off if they just could've managed to get a degree."

"You're probably right," Patrick replied. "But this isn't an easy decision for me."

Laura was relieved that she and Patrick could still have this level of discussion. With her work schedule and his travels, they didn't talk like they used to. She knew Pat was talented, and she also appreciated a formal education. In fact, she was studying for her graduate entrance exam but hadn't yet told anyone.

Perhaps Laura's talk with Pat would help him see the big picture. Sometimes it's hard to see the forest for the trees—even with a painter's eye.

Chapter 13

Estate Planning

Rich was seated at his desk in the home office reading an oil and gas industry magazine on the web when the phone rang. The caller ID indicated it was their good friend Roxanne, but Rich didn't bother to check it because the odds were that the call was for Peg. The calls were always for her, it seemed.

The dark wood office where Rich sat looked like an old library one would see in Europe, maybe even in a castle. As she hung up, Peg entered the office.

"Rich, I have some bad news," she said in a faltering voice. "That was Roxanne. Ernie's dead. He collapsed at home this morning and died before they got him to the hospital. It was a heart attack."

Rich was stunned. Peg took a seat next to him.

"I just can't believe it," she muttered.

Rich felt grief bearing down on his chest.

Ernie was 65. Only a few months before, they had been fishing together in Jackson Hole. Rich thought back to the trip and Ernie's behavior. Ernie had been his jovial and feisty self. He was definitely out of shape, his stomach big and round, and he lost his breath easily. But Ernie had been out of shape for decades. It never occurred to Rich his friend was on death's door.

"I can't believe it, either," Rich said holding Peg's hand tightly. "I just saw him the other day and he seemed fine. We had such a good time in Jackson Hole.

"How's Roxanne holding up?"

Roxanne was Ernie's first wife, and Skip's mother. She and Ernie had divorced 25 years ago, but she kept in contact with her ex-husband and paid attention to his well-being. Roxanne now lived in Santa Fe, where she owned an art gallery. Rich and Peg always enjoyed her company.

"She was pretty shaken up," Peg said. "Apparently Skip is here in Houston staying at Ernie's. He called 911 when Ernie collapsed, and then he called Roxanne. She's catching a flight to come to Houston tomorrow morning."

"I wonder what Skip is up to now," Rich said. "Should we try to find him and see how he's doing?"

"I don't know," Peg replied. "Roxanne said he was pretty upset. But he was helping make arrangements with the funeral home earlier this morning. She was worried he would probably disappear and go on a bender."

"That seems like a pretty harsh assessment," Rich said. "But I guess Skip has developed that reputation for himself.

"Well, at least he'll be taken care of financially," Rich added. "Ernie told me that he set up a trust for Skip, and Roxanne would be in charge of it. He feared Skip could get in some real trouble with a windfall of cash dumped in his lap."

"Not to mention the fact that most of it would be gone in a matter of months," Peg said. "Let's drive by Ernie's house and see if there's anything we can do."

She thought perhaps they could help, and she knew that would help Rich deal with his sudden loss.

Rich and Peg drove the 10 miles to Ernie's neighborhood in silence. Rich cried a little bit, thinking about his good-hearted friend and all the experiences they'd shared over the years.

There was the time Ernie booked them a tee time at Pebble Beach in California. Rich never cared much for golf, so it didn't make sense to spend $400 to play the game for a few hours. But Ernie made it fun with his good-natured intensity.

There was the time when Ernie had come along on a Viva family ski trip to Vail. Rich and Ernie rented cross-country skis one day and got lost on some remote trail. They didn't make it home until 8 p.m., just as Peg had gotten so worried that she was about to dial the police to send out a search party.

Rich also thought about the recent trip to Jackson Hole and how Ernie had felt so strongly about trying to explain financial planning to his newly retired friend. Yes, Ernie sometimes made things hard for himself—especially with women—but he loved his friends and would do anything to help them.

It was getting dark when they pulled up to Ernie's house. The driveway was empty, and the house looked mostly dark. Rich knocked on the door. Nobody answered.

"Skip is probably out doing his own thing," Rich said.

"It's sad to think the place is just empty," Peg responded as they turned to leave.

"I guess that's what we should have expected," Rich said. "Ernie lived alone."

They headed back toward home, stopping by Hunan Inn to get some take-out Chinese. After dinner they spent the evening looking through some old photo albums. There were several pictures of Ernie. Some showed him smiling and goofing around with Patrick and Laura. Often there was a different girlfriend on his arm at parties and dinners.

"You never could accuse Ernie of sleeping through life," Rich remarked.

Funerals have a strange way of bringing together people who normally would feel more comfortable simply exchanging holiday greeting cards.

The interment at Memorial Oaks Cemetery was for immediate family and close friends. Rich served as a pallbearer. He was honored to participate, although the intimacy of the event brought his sadness to the surface.

Following the burial, the small group of family and close friends made their way to St. Martin's Episcopal Church. A crowd of about 300 people had begun to gather for Ernie's memorial service. Since he died relatively young, there were lots of old friends and business colleagues still around to come pay their respects. The family row up-front was made up of Skip; his mom, Roxanne; Roxanne's second husband, Don; Ernie's second ex-wife, Cheryl; Cheryl's new husband, Bob; and Amelia, Ernie's girlfriend for the previous six months.

Rich thought to himself how Ernie would have been surprised to see this awkward group together at his funeral.

The service was short and dignified, and was followed by a reception.

Afterward, Rich and Peg had lunch with Roxanne at Ciao Bello, a nearby Italian food restaurant. They were in a solemn mood, but their memories and stories of good times with Ernie brought a few smiles. They also talked about what was going on in their lives.

"I wish Don and Skip could have joined us for lunch, Roxanne," Peg said.

"They volunteered to handle some of the takedown after the post-funeral reception at the church," Roxanne said. "We thought it would be good for Skip to have a project. We're worried about how he's going to handle all of this."

"When we were fishing in Jackson Hole a few months ago, Ernie shared with me that he had arranged for a trust to be established for Skip when Ernie died. He said you agreed to serve as the trustee," Rich said. "So at least you don't have to worry about him blowing through Ernie's life savings."

"Unfortunately, there's a bit of a snag with this," Roxanne informed them.

"What went wrong?" Rich inquired. "Ernie seemed certain that this was all taken care of."

"Fortunately, most of the assets are going into a trust for Skip. Ernie and I discussed this at length," Roxanne said. "But I've learned some additional information in the past few days from talking with the attorneys. It turns out that Ernie didn't list the trust as the beneficiary of his retirement accounts, nor his life insurance. As a result,

Skip will have complete control over the money in those accounts, and they're almost a third of Ernie's estate."

"Goodness, Roxanne, that doesn't sound good!" Peg said.

"Believe it or not, I'm more concerned about the cash causing problems for Skip than about him losing it all," Roxanne said. "Losing a third of Ernie's life savings would be bad enough, but blowing it on drugs and alcohol and partying would be even worse. Poor Ernie worked so hard to come up with a plan."

Retirement accounts, life insurance policies, and annuities pass to the beneficiaries listed on the respective documents. The documents are contracts, and therefore the assets in these instruments pass via beneficiary, and not through probate or wills. It's a good idea to review beneficiary designations every once in a while to make sure the information is accurate and up-to-date. In Ernie's case, it was doubtful that he had checked his beneficiary information for quite a while.

Ernie's wishes would have been carried out if he had indicated that the beneficiaries of his individual retirement account (IRA) and life insurance policy were to be determined by his last will and testament. The same holds true for annuities. The advantage of this approach is that the account holder may be more likely to maintain an updated will than updated beneficiary data on old retirement accounts and insurance policies.

In many cases, an investor wishes to bequeath assets to an individual person, not a trust, and does so by listing this person as beneficiary. In this case it is also advisable to designate contingent beneficiaries. This helps resolve inheritance questions if the primary beneficiary dies before the account owner, or if the two die simultaneously in an accident. Specifying contingent beneficiaries also gives the primary beneficiary the option of "disclaiming" assets so that they flow down to the contingent beneficiary or beneficiaries.

Rich thought about his estate planning situation for a moment. The Vivas had written their wills years before, but he hadn't paid much attention to estate planning other than that. He also wondered if he had any contingent beneficiaries listed on his retirement account. If he passed away and Peg didn't need the money from the retirement account, this would allow her to disclaim the assets and pass them to the contingent beneficiaries, Laura and Patrick. His thoughts turned back to Ernie.

"What are you going to do?" Rich asked Roxanne.

"Well, I'll certainly do my best at managing the part of the estate going into the trust, and I'm going to encourage Skip to let me help him with the portion he's responsible for," Roxanne said.

"Skip's not dumb, just irresponsible," she added. "If someone can convince him of the benefits of letting the IRA grow over time, perhaps he will listen to them and not withdraw all of it."

Ernie's IRA would be converted to a beneficiary IRA. This means that Skip would be required to take mandatory distributions each year. The distributions are taxed as ordinary income. However, the amount remaining in the IRA continues to grow tax-deferred if left within the IRA.

Ernie's mistake of leaving his retirement account and insurance proceeds outright to Skip was significant, and it did not meet the intent of his estate plan. However, in this case, at least the total going to Skip amounted to approximately one-third of his total estate, while two-thirds were going into a trust on Skip's behalf.

In some cases, the largest asset for an investor is the retirement account. Imagine how upsetting it would be to go through the estate planning process only for it to fall apart because the beneficiaries were listed incorrectly. A mistake in this situation could be devastating to an estate plan and result in a radically different outcome than what was intended by the decedent.

Rich, Peg, and Roxanne finished their lunch at Ciao Bello. Roxanne had to run to meet up with Don, her husband, and Skip.

"Good luck," Peg said as they departed. "Call us if you need anything."

They all hugged, wished each other well, and promised it would not be so long before they saw one another again.

Rich and Peg stopped to do some shopping at the grocery store and headed toward home.

"This is a wake-up call," Rich said to Peg. "I've been thinking so much about our financial plan, but we haven't revisited our wills for over five years, much less since we sold the business."

"If a planning mistake can happen to Ernie, it could happen to anyone. The bizarre part is Ernie knew more about investing than just about anyone we know. Unfortunately, Skip may pay the price for Ernie's estate planning mistake," Peg said.

"That is, if he blows it all," Rich said.

"I feel confident our beneficiaries haven't changed, but I don't know if we have contingent beneficiaries listed," Rich said. "Besides, almost everything else has changed in our life. We no longer own the business, but we have a lot more money to worry about now."

"It definitely fits in with the goals and objectives that we outlined in our financial plan," Peg said. "We've been talking about saving money for the kids and so forth. I can think of a million things I'd rather do, but we should probably make an appointment with an estate planning attorney and get our house in order."

They began talking about their assets. Their net worth was about $16 million, including the profit cleared on the business sale and their other assets, including their home and other savings.

"I don't pretend to understand the first thing about estate laws," Rich said. "I've heard they change a lot, with the political argument over the death tax and such. My main concern is that I don't want to let it get away from me, like Ernie accidentally did. We need to think again about how we want to leave our money to our kids. We've worked too hard and made too many sacrifices over the years to simply have all this evaporate in taxes after we die."

"I don't know how it works either, but I know there are definitely ways to plan beyond our deaths, and I don't think we've made the most of those," Peg said. "Our lives are different from Ernie's, but I'm sure there's still room for improvement in our wills."

When they got home, Rich e-mailed Greg's former assistant, who was now working with another advisor at Greg's firm, asking for a reference for an estate planning attorney. Then Rich went to the garage and pulled his fly rod from a jumble of equipment in the corner. He went to the yard and cast his line across the grass. He thought about fly fishing in Jackson Hole, and he remembered his good friend Ernie.

Later that week, Rich and Peg drove to the office of Scott Morrison and Dan Daly, estate planning attorneys who had been highly recommended by Greg's firm.

"Thanks for having us," Rich said as they greeted Scott. "We hadn't thought about estate planning for years, and then all of a sudden it seemed like we couldn't address it soon enough."

Scott chuckled. "That's surprisingly common. Did you have a medical scare? Or did one of your peers pass away? I hope you don't mind me asking."

"You nailed it," Peg replied. "Our longtime friend Ernie died from a heart attack last week. He was 65. It was pretty shocking to everyone."

"Well, it's often a wake-up call like that that spurs people to revisit their wills and estate plans," Scott said.

Scott ushered the Vivas into a conference room. "If it's okay with you, I'd like to start with a little presentation to set the groundwork for our discussion."

Scott's presentation started with the three types of taxes associated with estate planning: the estate tax, the gift tax, and the generation-skipping transfer tax. The estate tax is levied on assets transferred from a person to his or her beneficiaries at death. The gift tax is levied on assets passed during life. And the generation-skipping tax is levied when a donor transfers assets directly to grandchildren, or to someone more than 37.5 years younger. Each type of tax allows a certain amount of assets to transfer tax-free, known as the exclusion amount. The exclusion amount has changed considerably over the years, as has the tax rate applied on the amounts over the exclusion.

"The good news is that leaving assets from one spouse to another is tax-free," Scott added. "At least until the surviving spouse dies.

"Let's take your example. You've got a net worth of $16 million. If Rich dies first, which is typically the case because women tend to live longer than men, then he could leave everything to Peg. This is often referred to as an 'I love you will.'"

Peg giggled at the term, while Rich squirmed in his seat, feeling a bit unnerved by the prospect of his own death.

"You wouldn't owe any estate taxes at the time of the Rich's death," Scott continued. "However, when Peg dies, your heirs will pay taxes on everything above the exclusion amount."

Scott jotted down some figures. Today the exclusion amount is $5 million. Therefore for a couple, there would be a $10 million exclusion. That means the government would tax Rich and Peg's remaining $6 million at today's estate tax rate of 35 percent. That works out to a tax bill of $2.1 million, which would be due nine months after Peg's death.

"That's hard to swallow," Rich said, shaking his head at the idea that the government would be able to take a considerable portion of their net worth just because they died—especially since much of their net worth had already been taxed during their life though income taxes and capital gains taxes.

"It is, but there are ways of trying to minimize the tax burden," Scott said. "Rather than just leaving everything from one spouse to the other, many couples decide to create a bypass trust."

A bypass trust allows both husband and wife to take full advantage of the exclusion amount. When someone dies, the part of the estate not subject to tax is passed to a trust. Since Congress changes the dollar amount of the exclusion fairly often, it's a good idea to specify that the trust should receive the maximum amount permitted by the law, rather than a fixed dollar amount. In many cases, the surviving spouse still has full access to the funds within the bypass trust.

One of the true advantages of this arrangement is that the deceased spouse can dictate to whom the property passes at the death of the surviving spouse. This is important, because many prefer their assets to be used to the benefit of their surviving spouse and children. This way, regardless of whether the surviving spouse remarries, the wishes of the first decedent can still be carried out.

There was a time when, without a bypass trust, heirs would not get exclusions on both of their respective lives because their assets would flow directly to the spouse, without the heirs getting the exclusion on the first decedent's estate. Due to the portability concept, this is no longer the case.

"Then why go through the hassle of creating a bypass trust if the taxation ends up being the same?" Rich asked.

"There are a few reasons," Scott replied. "To begin with, the concept of portability expires at the end of 2012, unless extended by Congress. The main issue is so you can still maintain some control over your estate after your death—or 'manage from the grave,' as we like to say. If you pass away before your spouse, the trust allows you to dictate what happens to the assets in the trust after your spouse dies. This is particularly important should Peg remarry after your death. This is even more important should her new husband have children from a prior marriage."

"That makes a lot of sense," Peg said. "Why doesn't everybody do that?"

"Most people who have enough money to worry about this kind of thing do set up bypass trusts," Scott said.

"Without a doubt it sounds like a good idea to me," Rich said. "But it still doesn't make sense to me. If we take financial risks and sacrifice our time to build a business, and then we actually grow it into something of value, the government wants to tax us at our death. We've already paid taxes on all of our income and on the sale of the company. How is that fair? If the government taxes inheritance so much, would we be better off just giving our money away while we're still alive?"

"The IRS is one step ahead of you on that one," Scott replied. "Just like there are limits to the exemptions in the estate tax, there are also limits on the amount you can gift without incurring taxation."

Someone who wants to gift money to others without tax implications is limited to a certain amount. As of 2012, the amount was $13,000 per recipient per year. So, between Peg and Rich, they could give $26,000 to Patrick and another $26,000 to Laura without it being deemed a taxable gift. Rich and Peg could also give the same amount to their grandchildren or anyone else; the law doesn't say the recipient must be a relative.

"Generally, someone who's going this route generally is trying to pass money to their heirs tax-free and reduce the size of their estate to reduce their potential tax liability at death," Scott said.

"There's another element of gifting to consider," Scott added. "It's called the lifetime gift exclusion."

The lifetime gift exclusion is the total amount that a donor can give over his or her lifetime without being taxed. Congress changes the lifetime gift exclusion from time to time. As of 2012, the limit is set at $5 million. That means a couple can gift up to $10 million in their lifetime, across any number of recipients, without paying tax on the gift. Oftentimes the gift is made to a trust. If the assets in the trust grow, they do so outside of the donor's estate.

"How does the $13,000 annual limit factor into the lifetime gift exclusion?" Peg asked.

"Good question," Scott replied. "It means you can only give away a certain level each year—this year, it's $13,000 per recipient—and anything above that counts toward the lifetime gift exclusion."

Rich and Peg sat quietly for a moment, soaking in the information. Rich turned to Peg and brought up a related point.

"I guess we need to make certain that your mom doesn't list us in her will," he said. "It would make more sense for her to leave her estate to the kids as beneficiaries instead. I'm assuming her assets would fall below the exclusion amount, but odds are whatever we have will be above that amount. No need in making our death tax any larger than need be."

Scott shook his head and sighed. "Your line of thinking is smart, so I hate to be a wet blanket. Unfortunately the IRS also has a tax called the generation-skipping tax."

The generation-skipping tax kicks in when a grandchild or someone non-related that is 37.5 years younger than the donor inherits assets that were exempted from taxes when the grandparent—the donor in this case—transferred the assets to the grandchild.

"This applies to both the tax at death and to the tax on gifts above the annual exclusion, when a generation is skipped," Scott said.

"This is starting to make my head spin," Peg said.

"Well, that's why my job exists," Scott said. "If it was easy and everyone could handle this by themselves, I would have to find another line of work. But you shouldn't be discouraged. We can establish trusts for both of you to help transfer your wealth as efficiently as possible upon your death.

"Another thing to keep in mind is that trusts not only help minimize the tax burden on your estate, but they can also insulate the inheritance left for your heirs from lawsuits or divorce troubles," Scott added. "Trusts can also dictate certain terms, such as the age at which a child can become self-trustee, and in some cases, may even stipulate what is done with the assets."

"Ernie could definitely have benefited from that," Rich said to Peg.

Peg explained to Scott. "Ernie's our friend who recently passed last week. His death motivated us to set up this meeting and improve our estate planning. Ernie's son, Skip, is a bit of a ne'er-do-well, and everybody's worried that he's going to waste the portion of his inheritance that's not held in a trust."

"Without knowing about the specifics of that situation, I can tell you that there are ways to set up trusts to try to protect the assets while still passing them to the next generation. For example, you can appoint a trustee that has power over the trust to invest the assets, make distributions, and try to make sure the money lasts. Trustees can even change the age at which beneficiaries are allowed to withdraw from the trust on their own."

"I would hope we don't have to put that kind of leash on our children," Rich said. "But it's definitely worth thinking about. I'll tell you this: Ernie was a great friend. He taught me a lot about financial planning, and even though he's gone, he's still teaching us today."

Epilogue

R ich Viva had been on an interesting journey since selling Apex Compression Services. His initial jubilation was quickly overshadowed by the realization that he would no longer have the comfort and safety of regular income. His concerns may have been somewhat irrational, but they were also natural. For the first time in his adult life he was forced to contemplate his financial future in a way that he had been far too busy to worry about before.

With time on his hands, Rich couldn't help but question the meaning and purpose of his professional life. He regretted some of the sacrifices he'd made along the way, such as sacrificing time with family and friends at the expense of business priorities. But he also realized that he'd helped many people along the way: his customers, his employees, the domestic energy industry, and his family. Rich was also proud of his financial success, and he wanted to make the most of the next phase of life.

Rich had always been a goal-setter, and he felt compelled to make a plan for his retirement years, especially an investment plan. Some learn by reading, others by experience, and others by example. Rich counted on all three, and over time he had found examples all around him of people who had succeeded or failed at different aspects of investment planning. Those examples helped shape his approach to setting financial goals and objectives for the remainder of his and Peg's lives.

- **Greg Webber.** Greg was a top-notch financial advisor held in high esteem by all of his clients and colleagues. He wasn't clairvoyant, but his clients knew he was there for them and that he always did his best to offer the most helpful advice and guidance possible. However, Greg had failed in one aspect, and that was enjoying life each day. He was fulfilled by his laser focus on financial planning, but it also created stress for his family life and his health. His stress and single-mindedness surely contributed to his premature death at age 55 from a heart attack. Ultimately, Greg's failure to take care of his own well-being meant that he was not there to assist others at a time when they needed it most.
- **Ernie Troutman.** Ernie loved life to the extreme. Like Greg, his life came to an end too soon, but he definitely lived each day to the fullest. Ernie's biggest regret was not spending more time with his son, Skip, when the boy was in his formative years. If he'd provided more structure and discipline for Skip, and been a better role model, perhaps the boy would have learned to make better choices. As he grew older, Ernie learned the truth of the old adage that a parent is only as happy as his child.

  Ernie had excelled at financial planning in most respects. He'd provided well for his family and his heirs. Ernie's experience and knowledge helped Rich transition into retirement. Ernie taught Rich that a good financial plan could help alleviate many of life's concerns during the golden years. Ernie's caring and friendly demeanor had helped many over the years, but unfortunately his concern for Skip turned out to be too little and too late.
- **Roxanne.** Roxanne took her responsibility as trustee for Skip's inheritance seriously. Skip was unmanageable in so many ways that she appreciated the chance to make a difference in his life by doing her best to manage his trust. Through careful planning with

a financial advisor, the trust grew in value under Roxanne's management. Her well-designed allocation model provided both growth and income over time and was building to a point that, with continued monitoring and adjustment, should not only outlive her son but another generation or two.

- **Skip Troutman.** Like his father before him, Skip had a thirst for fun and excitement. However, Skip didn't share his father's work ethic, nor his investment acumen. It was fair to say that Skip took the party too far. He continued to battle alcoholism and cocaine abuse after his father died.

Skip's Hollywood experience never lived up to his dreams. Within a few months of Ernie's death, he decided to use his inheritance to produce his own movie and, hopefully, jump-start his stalled career in the movie industry. The movie—a B-rate horror film set on a houseboat at a Malibu marina—was a flop, even though Skip had a good time making it. He found that there were plenty of "friends" to help him in the pursuit, which was essentially a nonstop party.

Roxanne was encouraged that Skip had decided to put the money toward a project, rather than just spending it on consumables. Ernie had been a risk-taker, and maybe the movie project would pay off for Skip in the same way. It didn't happen that way, unfortunately. Within two years, he'd run through the portion of his inheritance that he could access.

Skip found that his so-called friends were quick to abandon him when the money was gone. At age 38, he was dependent upon the monthly stipend he received from the trust. He spent the money mostly on drugs and booze. Roxanne did what she could. She convinced Skip more than once to check into treatment centers, but sobriety never stuck. When he was sober, Skip couldn't help but dwell on his foolishness with his father's money. The regret and demoralization pushed him back to drugs and alcohol. On a cold December night during a visit to his mother's home in Santa Fe, Skip got his hands on some tainted heroin at a nightclub. The police found his body, nearly frozen, on a park bench on the outskirts of town. His trust was secure and thriving, but it no longer mattered at that point.

When people come into money quickly and haven't had the opportunity to prepare, the story often ends badly. Not all of them become addicted to drugs or alcohol, nor do all of them wreck their lives. But many find it difficult to make investment decisions because they fear that if they lose the money, they'll never make it back. Too often, the children of financially successful people don't have the ability to succeed as their parents did because the children were brought up differently. Their sense of entitlement, lack of work ethic, or fear of failure may cause them constant anxiety or worse, as was the case with Skip.

Family dynamics should be part of an investment plan. Financially successful people can find ways to instill a hard work ethic in their children and allow the children to have their own sense of value and meaning. Money alone doesn't do it. Finding a way to incentivize children to make decisions—especially investment decisions early in life—gives them a sense of accomplishment. When it comes time for these children to inherit assets, then they're able to take their family's wealth and turn it into something even more meaningful. Establishing a trust can make a big difference in a child's success and well-being for life.

- **Sally Victor.** Sally continued to volunteer in national parks for almost another decade until her health worsened. Over this same time period, Sally created her own foundation for environmental study and preservation. She made a generous contribution to her foundation and then worked tirelessly to raise additional funds for the cause. Sally's conversation with Rich and Peg at the lodge over coffee, and her efforts to teach financial concepts to her grandson Justin, rekindled her interest in investing. This time, she dedicated her financial prowess almost exclusively to her foundation, rather than a Wall Street firm or her family's financial well-being.

    In addition to founding and chairing the Victor Foundation, Sally also chaired the foundation's investment committee. There, she was able to bring her understanding of investing and her love of nature together. She used both passions to drive her to build an endowment that would last for generations to come. Sally succeeded at her goal. The foundation funded school programs that taught following generations about the natural world and environmental preservation. Many people would be happy to have one meaningful and successful career; Sally could honestly claim two. She came to embody what Rich hoped to achieve: a meaningful life after retirement.

- **Justin Victor.** Sally's legacy also included her grandson, Justin, and the lessons she taught him about financial investing. He not only understood investment concepts, but also appreciated how they might help him with his own financial situation. His grandmother's lectures gave him a deeper understanding of business and the economic world than a typical environmental science graduate.

  Justin went on to pursue a career in forestry and found work at a timber company for which his grandmother served on the board of directors. Justin enjoyed the work and was blessed with the same work ethic that made his grandmother a success. Justin quickly moved into an entry-level management position and within a few years had worked his way up the ladder to a mid-level executive position.

  Sally continued to coach Justin, and she was proud of the progress he was making professionally. She offered him a seat on the Victor Foundation's board, for she saw that he shared a passion for nature and was growing into a good businessman and investor. Justin's work on the nonprofit board didn't go unnoticed. Not long after joining the board, a securities analyst who worked for the same firm as one of Justin's fellow board members reached out to see if he would be interested in joining the investment firm as a research associate.

  Justin thought about the opportunity and asked Sally for advice. Sally presented the pros and cons of this possible career shift but in the end left it to her grandson to make his decision. "You've got a good head on your shoulders, Justin. You'll figure it out," is about all she would say.

  Justin was surprised at his grandmother's uncharacteristic reticence, but he realized it was time for him to chart his own path.

- **Lucille Sharpwell**, Rich's 10th-grade math teacher. Lucille and Johnny Sharpwell continued to live a comfortable life in retirement. When they weren't traveling, you could find them playing golf almost daily at the country club located in the subdivision where they lived. They continued with a diversified investment approach and were comfortable with their decisions, which provided them peace and security as they grew older together.

- **Martha Hamilton**, Rich's high school history teacher. Martha became increasingly worried over money as the value of her savings dwindled as a result of inflation and lack of investment return. Old age was not good for Martha. She couldn't cut back any more than she already had. She was living a miserly life, but she still had a few CDs in the bank. She monitored the CDs like a hawk, constantly moving money from one bank to another to get a fraction of a percentage point more in interest. Partly because of her fear of investing, she had outlived her savings. Life would have been much better had she applied a more balanced approach to money management.

- **Judy Kenneth**, Rich's high school biology teacher. Judy continued to work into her early 80s, because she had to pay the bills. Judy had always retained her gambling spirit—the same risk tolerance that gave her the courage to pick up and move to Houston by herself as a young woman—but the approach never seemed to pan out financially. Each time she developed a small amount in savings, she would risk it all in the next idea to make her millions. She was still looking for the latest "strike it rich" idea. None was to be found.

- **Will Frederick**, master winemaker at Shady Oaks Vineyard. Each year, Will made subtle changes to Shady's Secret Meritage, the winery's most popular label, but he never deviated substantially from the careful blend that stood the test of time. Will's changes at the margins made the wine better, and the label never lost its integrity. Will couldn't imagine giving up his life as a winemaker in Sonoma County, and he probably never would.

- **Larry Montclair**, owner of Frais Valley Vineyard. Larry loved his work at Frais Valley, and the vineyard prospered under his ownership. After years of success, he no longer worried about his winery's survival, but he still continued to be an active financial investor. He had already been approached by two larger wineries to sell, but had declined both opportunities. He didn't need the money, and he was having too much fun as owner and winemaker of Frais Valley.

- **Habib**, the taxi driver in Boston. Habib continued to work as a taxi driver for a few more years before his wife and children convinced him to retire at age 65. Habib's investments had not been in stocks or bonds, but in his children and their education. Habib and his wife lived a simple life with few expenses. They had a loving family, and their children were thriving in the United States. Each had graduated from college and was pursuing an interesting career. His three children were now taking care of Habib and his wife. Fortunately for him, all three loved and respected their parents, and did not turn their back on them as the tables had turned. Habib was a rich man indeed.

- **Tom Pepperdino**, the baseball enthusiast. Tom fulfilled his goal of attending at least one game in every Major League Baseball park within a couple of years. He enjoyed attending the games, but the true joy came from the opportunity to travel and see different parts of the country. Tom's cash flow ladder provided a sense of security regardless of market uncertainties, and therefore he was never worried about his travel expenses. He had harvested gains along the way to replenish the cash flow ladder as needed.

  After completing the ballpark tour, Tom and his wife decided to take on a similar, but even bigger adventure. The two set the goal of visiting every capitol building in the United States. Tom's wife also tried to see as many governor's mansions as possible after reading Cathy Keating's book *Our Governors' Mansions*. Three years into the project, they had already visited 10 states. Their goal provided an excuse to travel the country, and their cash flow ladder gave them the ability to do so.

- **Reverend Jim Conroy.** Reverend Conroy and Rich kept up their friendship and regular breakfasts at the Houstonian. On more than one occasion, Reverend Conroy provided useful guidance to Rich in his new life in retirement. For his part, Rich kept his position on the church's business council, and volunteered many hours and much business insight to the church's well-being. After a few years, Reverend Conroy was forced to retire from active church duties because of the church's mandatory retirement age. Regardless of employment status, the two would remain friends for life.

Shortly after Reverend Conroy's retirement, Rich called to invite him along for a fly fishing trip to Jackson Hole. Rich was hoping that perhaps he could help his friend in the same way that Ernie had done for him. As the plane landed, Rich leaned over and said, "Welcome to paradise, Jim," and smiled as he thought of Ernie. Although Reverend Conroy was not in the same state of bewilderment that Rich had experienced immediately after retiring, he would still need a good friend during his transition.

- **Fred Burdon.** Intellectually, Fred knew that reacting to gyrations in the market rarely paid off over the long term. Psychologically, he had a hard time controlling himself. Fred learned this the hard way after selling 80 percent of his equity holdings near the market bottom of 2009. His financial advisor attempted to provide enough background, logic, and investment metrics to prevent Fred from making such kneejerk reactions. But Fred went with his gut, and decided to leave 20 percent of his portfolio at risk and liquidate the other 80 percent. It proved to be a bad move. The market recovered significantly, but only 20 percent of Fred's holdings went up. The remainder was sitting in cash.

Fred was a smart guy, but he was vulnerable to market hype and volatility. He didn't want to do anything stupid, and as a result immersed himself in the markets. He interpreted each minor news announcement as a major event.

Over the previous 30 years, the average intra-year pullback from peak to trough was 15 percent. This didn't calm Fred when the markets experienced a 19-percent drop from peak to trough in 2011. Fred liquidated half of his holdings, but convinced himself to keep half in the market, because he remembered what happened to him in 2009. But then a shift occurred, and the markets roared back. Within five months of liquidating half of his portfolio, the markets had made up the entire loss and had even rallied an additional 10 percent. Fearing the market was about to take a major run up, he bought back in with the half he had previously liquidated, in effect buying at a 30-percent premium to where he had liquidated only a few months before. Fred felt like a real fool, but found himself repeating the same mistakes over and over again.

Some time later, when the markets had calmed and Fred didn't feel as if he was in the heat of battle, he would realize his mistakes and attempt to change. Fortunately for Fred, he had a significant net worth with which to work. Unfortunately, he would have had considerably more had he simply stopped confusing the noise with the news.

Fred, the fun, charismatic guy who everyone loved, became so shortsighted, myopic, and obsessed with investing that he alienated those around him. In the end, very few people were willing to keep Fred as a friend. He was simply too draining to spend more than short periods of time with. Deep down, Fred knew what was happening, but for some reason he was unable to learn the lesson. Fred's preoccupation with the "noise" cost Fred financially and personally. His golden years ended up less than golden.

- **Tim Ida.** Like Fred, Tim was an overactive investor. But unlike Fred, Tim didn't have trouble differentiating between news and noise. Tim's investment fault was that he was simply bored. He felt he should always be doing something. At times, Tim would even buy the very holding he had just sold days before. If he had made significant profits, perhaps he could justify the activity, but often the transactions had no rhyme or reason.

Before the tech bubble in the late 1990s, Tim would have enjoyed day trading. People were actually leaving their day jobs to trade in and out of securities with the goal of making a few pennies per share on a trade. There were locations referred to as trading rooms where they would rent space to trade stocks. When the markets turned south, many of these people were wiped out. Fortunately for Tim, he was too busy running his various businesses at the time and didn't get into day trading. Tim was an active trader but not as active as the old day traders once were.

Tim was never wiped out, but he would have had much better investment results had he invested with a strategy based on logic and reason, and not because he needed a distraction to occupy his day. Tim's love for constant movement would prevent him from ever realizing significant gains in his investment portfolio.

- **The Vivas.** After spending Christmas and New Year's at home with his parents, Patrick Viva decided to return to Paris, despite his parents' urging to return to college at LSU. Patrick appreciated his parents' concerns and their offer to start an investment account for him. But he also felt they never fully understood the importance of living and studying art in Paris.

Back in Paris, Patrick had to make it on his own. He soon learned that without money from his parents, it was tough to make a living by selling an occasional painting and washing dishes. Patrick felt he was growing as a painter, but he also got tired of the constant struggle to make ends meet.

After about nine more months in Paris, Patrick made the call that Rich and Peg had been waiting for. He returned to the United States, and re-enrolled at LSU with a full load of classes. Patrick also took his parents up on the offer to start an investment fund. He put in the little money that he had, and his parents added a matching amount and then some.

By the time he completed his degree, Patrick had saved about $20,000 in his investment fund. He discussed various uses for the money, but in the end decided to pursue a graduate degree in art. He wanted to become a museum curator. It took five years, but Patrick eventually earned his Ph.D. in art studies. Patrick realized that had it not been for his parents' intervention and tough love, he could have been a dropout washing dishes, versus Dr. Viva. Patrick still enjoyed and aspired to one day create a painting worthy of the New York museum galleries where he worked.

Laura Viva continued to thrive professionally and personally. She excelled in her job at Exxon, and Rich and Peg had no doubt that she would continue to rise in the ranks there. That's why it was quite a surprise when Laura announced that she was leaving Exxon to start her own consulting company.

Laura's foundation for the new company was the investment fund that she had started with her parents' help about six years earlier. The fund provided the seed money she needed to get her consultancy off the ground. She knew the stakes were high, for few who retire from Exxon do so poorly. But like her dad, her entrepreneurial spirit was calling and she wanted to be the boss.

Rich and Peg served as ad hoc advisors to Laura as she opened Viva Petro Consulting. Patrick loaned her some of his paintings to hang on the walls of her small office, including one that he painted back in Paris. It didn't take long for Laura's business plan to take flight. In two years, her business was thriving, and she was honored as one of the top 40 executives in Houston under 40 years old.

The Vivas had plenty of reasons to be proud of both of their children. Both were doing well, but neither seemed to have much time for a significant love relationship. Peg longed for grandchildren one day and was ready to open 529 plans the moment they arrived.

After months of worry and stress, Rich had achieved a level of comfort with his financial planning and spent most of his days in contentment. A big part of his progress was the Vivas' selection of a financial advisor after taking months to find the right person at the right firm. The advisor they chose came highly recommended from an old friend and colleague of Rich's. The connection helped, because their relationship had an element of trust already established between their mutual friends.

Rich and Peg learned a tremendous amount about investment planning in the year following the business sale. They brought their knowledge to the table as they worked with their new advisor to develop an investment plan that matched their investment goals and objectives. Their spending levels still amazed Rich, but their advisor helped them establish a cash flow ladder so they didn't need to worry about every fluctuation in the markets.

Rich enjoyed working closely with his financial advisor. The two men had become friends as they met once or twice a year in person and talked on the phone regularly. They worked together to decide tactical moves and to reallocate the portfolio as necessary.

From time to time, the advisor suggested that the Vivas should harvest gains from specific parts of their portfolio that provided above-average returns. They used the harvested proceeds to re-plenish their cash flow ladder. It became a comfortable routine for the Vivas and helped build their confidence in their financial future.

By really thinking it through and taking his time at the outset, Rich was no longer second-guessing himself, and he didn't panic at the "noise" in the media's coverage of the markets—not that there hadn't been plenty of market pullbacks and surges over the years since he established the plan. But Rich had learned to pay attention to the important news and tune out the rest. He was a good investor.

Rich had achieved a level of contentment that would have seemed impossible immediately after the sale of ACS. He enjoyed making up for lost time with Peg. He also found plenty of outlets to stay engaged in the community. In addition to serving on the Grace Methodist business council, he had maintained a position on the board of the Association of Independent Oilfield Service Companies and wrote a column for the association's monthly newsletter.

Rich's retirement and sense of financial security were a relief for Peg. She had been looking forward to his retirement for years, but hadn't predicted the turmoil he would face after the business sale. Peg continued to monitor their investments a little more closely than Rich, using her natural financial sense to keep things on track. Peg and Rich were good sounding boards for one another as they contemplated their investment planning, along with their financial advisor.

Peg stayed involved in various charities but had relinquished her leadership roles over time. She still contributed to fundraising efforts for the causes important to her, but she left the heavy lifting to the younger volunteers. This year, Peg also chaired the ladies' fundraising luncheon event for TUTS, the musical theatre group in Houston that she and Rich had supported over the years.

After a couple of years of retirement, Rich and Peg made the leap and purchased a vacation home in Florida along the scenic 30A highway. They rented out the house when they weren't using it, and even made a little money on the deal. A year later, they also purchased a condo in Vail. Patrick and Laura used the Vail condo more in the winter, while Rich and Peg liked to visit in the summer to escape the Houston heat and humidity. They tended to spend the majority of the year in Houston, with summers in Vail and the fall in Florida. Rich and Peg also made frequent trips to New York to visit Patrick and catch major exhibits at the museums.

The vacation homes were nice, as were the financial security and productive investment portfolio. But more important than any of that for Peg and Rich were their loving relationship, successful children, and great quality of life. The Vivas didn't get overwhelmed with their investments because they had the wisdom to overlook the noise, a cash flow ladder to provide for their needs, and a relationship with their financial advisor to help keep everything on track. They thanked God daily for their blessings and for all those who entered their life along their journey to help show them the way.

About the Authors

John David "J.D." Joyce has been advising clients with their investments since 1993 and was named a Top Financial Advisor in the United States by *Barron's* in 2009, 2010, and 2011. He has assisted investors through their personal changes and various market cycles in his position as a financial and wealth advisor with the same major Wall Street firm throughout his career. Based on his experience successfully guiding clients, he has developed unique and insightful strategies and recommendations to help investors achieve their financial goals. In addition, he is a Guinness World Record holder for consecutive hours swinging in a hammock, set while raising funds for multiple sclerosis research. J.D. is actively involved in his community and church, and when not working with investments, he enjoys reading, writing, studying politics, traveling, running, bicycling, and spending time with his family. He resides in Houston with his wife and two children.

Matt Joyce is a journalist and writer who has worked in the news business in Texas, Wyoming, Colorado, and New Mexico. He prefers to be outdoors, spending time with his family, enjoying music and sports.

Index

A

ACS (Apex Compression Services, Inc.), 3–6, 9

Advisors, *see* Financial advisors

Alternative investments, 72, 91, 92

Annuities:
  in estate planning, 163
  variable, 90–91

Apex Compression Services, Inc. (ACS), 3–6, 9

Apple, 19

Assets:
  disclaiming, 163, 164
  in estate planning, 162–170

Asset allocation, 67–78
  asset classes in, 72
  defined, 72
  maintaining consistency with, 76–77
  matching goals with, 74
  necessity of, 73
  overview of, 19–20
  and variations in diversification, 76
  wine analogy, 67–72, 74, 76–77

Asset classes, 72, 75

Association of Independent Oilfield Service Companies, 95

B

Barclays Aggregate Bond Index, 84

Bartiromo, Maria, 21

Bear Stearns, 132

Beneficiaries, 163–165

Berra, Yogi, 16

Bible, 128–130, 132

Bonds, 72

Boston Marathon, 95–104

Budgeting, 42

Bush, George H.W., 126

Bypass trusts, 167–168

C

Cash, 72

Cash flow, 111–123
  as goal, 42
  and market crashes, 116–119
  overview of, 17–19

Cash flow (*cont'd*)
  and retirement, 116–117
  and spending, 119, 122
  and time horizon, 106, 107
Cash flow ladder, 17, 117–120,
  122
Certificates of deposit (CDs), 118
Charities, 49–50, 55
Cheney, Dick, 14
Children. *See also* Family
  inheritance by, 47–49, 106, 169.
    See also Estate planning
  investing for, 155–157
  talking about money with, 49
Closed-end funds, 90
Confidentiality, 130
Continental Airlines, 113
Contingent beheficiaries, 163–164
Creditworthiness, 91

D
Daily Catch (restaurant), The, 97
Derivatives, 91
Disclaiming assets, 163, 164
Diversification:
  in mutual funds, 90
  of portfolios, *see* Portfolio
    diversification
  of unit investment trusts, 91
  with variable annuities, 90–91
Donations, 49–50
Dow Jones Industrial Average (DJIA),
  84, 120
Dreams, 16

E
Earnings:
  PEG ratio, 85, 88–89
  P/E ratio, 85–87
  trailing, 85
Earnings per share (EPS), 85–86
Economic indicators, 83, 85–88

Enron, 115–116
Entrepreneurship, 3
EPS (earnings per share), 85–86
Equities, 63, 72
Equity market:
  March 2009 crash, 86–87
  news versus noise about, 145
Escalante's (restaurant), 135
Estate planning, 21, 159–170
  documents for, 163
  lifetime gift exclusion in, 168–169
  professional assistance for,
    165–166
  role of beneficiaries in, 163–165
  and sudden death, 160
  taxes associated with, 166–169
  with trusts, 162–163, 167–170
Estate tax, 166
Exchange-traded funds (ETFs), 90
Expenses, 41–42
Exxon Mobil Corp., 27–28, 180

F
Family, 16, 149–158
  and estate planning, 21. *See also*
    Estate planning
  investing for children, 155–157
  as part of investment planning,
    174
Financial advisors, 125–133
  characteristics of desirable,
    129–131
  confidentiality with, 130
  developing good relationships with,
    43
  good communication with, 129
  importance of choosing, 132
  level of trust with, 128
  researching, 131
  selection of, 20
Financial Industry Regulatory Authority
  (FINRA), 131

Index

Financial planning, 7–8. *See also* Investment plans
  529 plans, 48
Frais Valley, 80–81

G

General Electric, 19, 84
Generation-skipping tax, 166, 169
Gift exclusion, lifetime, 168–169
Gift tax, 166
Goals and objectives, 35–36, 39–51
  aligning strategy with, 38
  approaches to saving and investing in, 42–43
  cash flows in, 42
  and estimating expenses, 41–42
  financial advisors' understanding of, 129
  as first step in planning, 41
  and giving back, 49–50
  importance of, 40
  and inheritance, 47–49
  investment strategy in, 43–44
  matching asset allocation with, 74
  and talking to your children about money, 49
  and vacation homes, 45–47
Golden rule, 131
Grace Methodist Church, 49, 125
Grand Teton National Park, 30, 39
Growth companies, 88, 89
Growth stocks, 76

H

Hatfield Energy Corp., 62, 115
Hedging, 37
Heirs, 167, 169
Hierarchy of needs, 2
Houston Chronicle, 146
Houstonian (social club), 125–126
Houstonian Hotel, Club & Spa, 125
Hunan Inn (restaurant), 161

I

Individual retirement accounts (IRAs), 163, 164
Information:
  interpreting, *see* News versus noise
  short-term, 141
Inheritance, 47–49, 106, 169. *See also* Estate planning
Insurance, life, 163
Interpreting information, *see* News versus noise
Investing, 79–93
  economic indicators in, 83, 85–88
  lack of control over, 8
  referring to investment indices for, 83–84
  risk-taking in, 81
  vessels for, 90–92
  wine analogy, 82–83, 87–90
Investment indices, 83–84
Investment plans, ix, 13–25
  asset allocation in, 19–20
  cash flow, 17–19
  elements of, 16
  and estate planning, 21
  guidance with, xi
  news versus noise in, 21–22
  purpose of, 16
  risk tolerance in, 16–17
  role of family in, 174
Investment returns, 142
Investment strategy, 38, 43–44
Investor returns, 142
IRAs (individual retirement accounts), 163, 164

J

Jackson Hole, Wyoming, 13, 46
Jenny Lake Lodge, 30, 31

K

Keating, Cathy, 177
Keene, Tom, 21
K-1s, 91

L

Large-cap stocks, 19
Last will and testament, 163
Lehman Brothers, 91
Life insurance policies, 163
Lifetime gift exclusion, 168–169
Limited partnerships, 91
L'Osteria, 97, 98

M

Madoff, Bernie, 132
Market crashes:
    cash flow and, 116–119
    and projecting overall market, 86–87
Maslow, Abraham, 2
Master limited partnership (MLP),
    91–92
Memorial Oaks Cemetery, 161
Meritage, 68, 70, 76–77
Mid-cap stocks, 19
MLP (master limited partnership),
    91–92
Money:
    outliving your, 60, 62
    talking with children about, 49
Morgan Stanley Capital International
    Europe Australasia and Far East
    (MSCI EAFE) Index, 84
Mutual funds, 90, 92

N

Nasdaq Composite, 84
Nasdaq 100, 84
National parks, 32, 35–36
National Elk Refuge, 27
National Park Service, 32, 38
Needs, hierarchy of, 2
Net worth, 167

News versus noise, 135–147
    in equity markets, 145
    and exposure to bad news, 146
    and interpreting information, 141
    and investor returns, 142
    making distinction between, 140
    and obsessing over portfolio, 139–140
    overview of, 21–22
    and panic selling, 143–144
    and retirement, 136
Number 9 Park (restaurant), 98, 102

O

Objectives, *see* Goals and objectives
Olivette (restaurant), 125
Open-end funds, 90
Our Governors' Mansions (Cathy
    Keating), 177
Outliving your money, 60, 62

P

Panic selling, 143–144
Parenthood, 24
Partnerships, 91–92
PEG (price-to-earnings to growth)
    ratio, 85, 88–89
P/E (price-to-earnings) ratio, 85–87
Planning, 9. *See also* Investment plans
    estate planning, *see* Estate planning
    financial, 7–8
    goals and objectives in, 41
Portfolios:
    diversification of, 19, 62, 74–76.
        See also Asset allocation
    obsessing over, 139–140
    uniqueness of, 92, 93
Portfolio managers, 90
Price-to-earnings (P/E) ratio, 85–87
Price-to-earnings to growth (PEG)
    ratio, 85, 88–89

Q

QQQ (Nasdaq 100), 84

Index

R

Red River BBQ (restaurant), 56–57
Retirement, 9–10
  and cash flow, 116–117
  and news versus noise, 136
  Peg's rules for, 68
  stress during, 13
Retirement accounts, 163, 164
Returns:
  on investments, 142
  negative, 61
Risk:
  assessment of, 43
  defining, 36
  in investing, 81
  purpose of, 38
Risk tolerance, 53–65
  aggressive approach to, 62–64
  conservative approach to, 60,
    62
  defined, 54
  importance of, 71
  individual differences in, 59
  moderate approach to, 54, 59–60,
    64–65
  and negative returns, 61
  overview of, 16–17
Roosevelt, Theodore, 33
Russell 2000, 84

S

Segregated holdings, 92
Separately managed accounts (SMAs),
  92
Shady Oaks, 68–70, 74, 79
Short-term information, 141
Small-cap stocks, 19
SMAs (separately managed accounts),
  92
S&P (Standard & Poor's) 500, 44,
  83–87, 120
Spending, 119, 122
Stanford Financial, 132

Stocks:
  growth, 76
  large-cap, 19
  and likelihood of loss, 108
  mid-cap, 19
  small-cap, 19
  types of, 19
  value, 76
Stock market crashes, 85–87, 119–121,
  143
Structured products, 91

T

Tax(es), 91–92, 166–169
  estate, 166
  generation-skipping, 166, 169
  gift, 166
Tech bubble, 118, 179
Tech companies, 89
Time horizon, 95–109
  and cash flow, 106, 107
  external forces affecting, 106
  importance of, 109
  and inheritance, 106
  and likelihood of loss, 108
  marathon analogy, 95–107
Trailing earnings, 85
Travel, 68–69
Treasury securities, 63
Trusts:
  bypass, 167–168
  estate planning with, 162–163,
    167–170
  unit investment, 91
TUTS (Theatre Under The Stars),
  50

U

UITs (unit investment trusts),
  91
United Airlines, 113
U.S. Department of Agriculture,
  33

U.S. Forest Service, 32–33, 37, 38
U.S. Treasury securities, 63
Unit investment trusts (UITs), 91
Utility companies, 89

V
Vacation homes, 45–47, 182–183
Value companies, 88
Value stocks, 76
Variable annuities, 90–91

Viva Petro Consulting, 181
Volatility, 16, 36

W
White Mountain Creamery (restaurant), 99
Wills, 163

Y
Yellowstone National Park, 39

Stay in touch!

Subscribe to our free Finance and Accounting eNewsletters at
www.wiley.com/enewsletters

Visit our blog: **www.capitalexchangeblog.com**

 Follow us on Twitter
@wiley_finance

 "Like" us on Facebook
www.facebook.com/wileyglobalfinance

 Find us on LinkedIn
Wiley Global Finance Group

WILEY Global Finance
WHERE DATA FINDS DIRECTION